POLITICAL SCIENCE IN A NUTSHELL

THIRTY THINGS THAT WILL HELP YOU UNDERSTAND POLITICAL SCIENCE

—⚬—

BY

BRADLEY W. RASCH

CONTENTS

—𝔪—

INTRODUCTION

—ᘰᘰ—

Political Science is often defined in the following manner:
A social science concerned chiefly with the description and analysis of political and especially governmental institutions and processes.

An alternate definition might be:
An academic discipline concerned with the empirical study of government and politics.

Or:
A social science dealing with political institutions and with the principles and conduct of government.

Political scientists have investigated the nature of states, the roles and functions performed by various governments, voter behavior, political parties, political culture, political economy, and public opinion, and almost any manner of other topics. Though Political Science has roots in the political philosophies of Plato and Aristotle, political science in the modern sense did not begin until the 19th century, when many of the social sciences were first established. Before it was called Political Science, it was often referred to as Political Economy, highlighting the relationship between the two now independent disciplines. Its empirical and scientific orientation is traceable to the work of Auguste Comte and Henri de Saint-Simon. . The first institution dedicated to its study, the Free School of Political Science, was founded in Paris, France in 1871.

Woodrow Wilson once said:
The method of political science is the interpretation of life; its instrument is insight, a nice understanding of subtle, unformulated conditions.

Mark Twain stated:
"In religion and politics people's beliefs and convictions are in almost every case gotten at second-hand, and without examination, from authorities who have not themselves examined the questions at issue but have taken them at second-hand from other"

It is noted that Plato wrote:

"Those who are too smart to engage in politics are punished by being ruled by those who are dumber."

An unattributed saying about politics often quoted states that:
"Any 20 year-old who isn't a liberal doesn't have a heart, and any 40 year-old who isn't a conservative doesn't have a brain."

"Democracy means simply the bludgeoning of the people by the people for the people."- Oscar Wilde

This book will explain the thirty most important concepts of Political Science in a concise and straightforward style. The goal of this book is to give the reader an understanding of this vital and fascinating field.

PART I

WHO IS IN CHARGE?

1

DESPOTISM

—⚏—

Despotism is also called tyranny. One individual is in charge, and governs with little or no concern for the populace. That one person in charge may be called a Despot, Tyrant, or Dictator. This Dictator, or Tyrant (take your pick) typically has absolute power, and is not subject to the laws of the country he leads (they usually are he's, think Hitler and Saddam Hussein). In fact, his word is law. It is his way or the highway (or worse).

A Dictator sits at the head of what is often called a Totalitarian or Authoritarian state. Often, they justify their rule by adherence to some ideology, or by their ability to protect their country from some internal or external threat. This threat can be real or imagined, but if the people of the country believe in it, and fear it, the Dictator finds it easier to stay in power.

The key feature of Tyranny or Despotism is that the leader is above the law. John Locke famously said, "Wherever the law ends, Tyranny begins".

2

MONARCHY

Monarchs may be called King, Queen, Sheikh, Potentate, Emperor, or a number of other names. They generally come to their position by heredity; often they are the son or daughter of the previous Sovereign. For a long period of world history, they claimed that their authority to rule came from God, even in a country that was secular (not a theocracy). Eventually, most Monarchs dropped the claim that God willed their rule.

There was a time in history when Monarchs had a great deal of power, or shared it with other royalty (Dukes, Earls, and the like). Now, in most of the world, Monarchs are figureheads, and have little or no power. Their roles are largely ceremonial (as in The United Kingdom). Often, the people in their "Kingdom" have great affection for them. This affection for the Royalty is a form of patriotism to the state, and promotes a national unity. Countries with Kings, Queens and other such Monarchs are in fact governed by Parliaments, Prime Ministers, and other elected leaders. There are some exceptions in the modern world such as Saudi Arabia.

It is fair to say that "the King reigns, but does not govern".

3

ARISTOCRACY

Aristocracy has be defined in the following ways:

1. Government by the "best" citizens.

2. A ruling body composed of the "best" citizens.

3. A form a government, in which the supreme power is vested in the principal persons of a state, or in a privileged order; an oligarchy.

4. The nobles or chief persons in a state; a privileged class or patrician order; (in a popular use) those who are regarded as superior to the rest of the community, as in rank, fortune, or intellect.

Saying that it is the rule of the few can sum up aristocracy. Running a country is so complex and difficult that those in favor of Aristocracy justify it's very existence by suggesting that only the best and brightest are capable of, and therefore should, rule. Throughout history, Aristocrats have not always been the best and the brightest. Often they have obtained their positions by heredity. For Centuries, their most wealthy families have influenced nations. This too is part of what an Aristocracy is. Many people that sit in the United States Senate are millionaires. Though Aristocracy justifies itself as saying only the capable should rule, that there should be a Meritocracy of leadership, sadly, that is often not the case.

Thomas Jefferson said: "There is a natural aristocracy among men. The grounds of this are virtue and talents".

He also stated: "I hope we shall crush in its birth the aristocracy of our monied corporations which dare already to challenge our government to a trial by strength, and bid defiance to the laws of our country".

John Adams once said: "We are the only real aristocracy in the world: the aristocracy of money".

Is the United States in some sense an Aristocracy? Look at the wealth of those that have served as President, the financial resources of the people sitting in Congress, and the families that have sent multiple members to the halls of power: Bush, Kennedy, Clinton, Adams, and so on.

4

OLIGARCHY

An Oligarchy can be defined in the following manner:

Government by the few

A government in which a small group exercises control especially for corrupt and selfish purposes; *also*: a group exercising such control

Chris Hayes, in his recent book *Twilight Of The Elite* said the following about Oligarchies:

Those who are able to climb up the ladder will find ways to pull it up after them, or selectively lower it down to allow their friends, allies, and kin to scramble up. In other words: 'Who says meritocracy says oligarchy.'

Charles de Montesquieu stated:

The tyranny of a prince in an oligarchy is not so dangerous to the public welfare as the apathy of a citizen in a democracy.

Historically, Oligarchies have served to take from the people and give to the elite, those in control. As you have seen, an Aristocracy is also rule by the few. But an Aristocracy often rules for the common good, whereas an Oligarchy rules for the good of the few.

In an Oligarchy, the self-interest of the ruling class, the Oligarchs, is supreme. Both Economic and Military power is controlled by the privileged few, be they families, clans, or interest groups, and the number one priority is to stay in power so privilege is not lost.

There is little input from the common people in an Oligarchy, though the Oligarchs may go to great pains to make it appear as though there is.

In Oligarchies, dissent is often dealt with extremely harshly.

Here in the Western Hemisphere, especially in Latin America, there is a strong history of Oligarchies.

5

DEMOCRACY

—ᨏ—

A Democracy can best be defined as follows:

A government by the people; *especially*: rule of the majority

A government in which the supreme power is vested in the people and exercised by them directly or indirectly through a system of representation usually involving periodically held free elections

A political unit that has a democratic government

The common people especially when constituting the source of political authority

The absence of hereditary or arbitrary class distinctions or privileges

Abraham Lincoln may have best described a Democracy in his Gettysburg Address by describing it as "a government of the people, by the people, and for the people".

Not to split hairs, but the term Democracy and Republic are often used interchangeably, but they do not mean exactly the same thing. A Democracy suggests that all of the people make a nation's decisions. A Republic is similar, but there is a distinction. In a Republic, the people elect representatives that make decisions for the country. If one utilizes this distinction, the United States is technically a Republic, not a Democracy, though it is certainly democratic in nature. A true Democracy in a large nation is certainly not feasible.

As time has gone on, the two terms, Democracy and Republic have become synonymous and a distinction is no longer made between the two, as was once the case.

In human history, Democracy is relatively new. Though most of the nations on earth now call themselves Democracies, the quality of those Democracies vary. Certainly, even in our own nation, Democracy is evolving. Women were not always able to vote, for example.

Some prominent people have made some interesting observations about Democracy:

The best argument against democracy is a five-minute conversation with the average voter.
Winston Churchill

As I would not be a slave, so I would not be a master. This expresses my idea of democracy.
Abraham Lincoln

It has been said that democracy is the worst form of government except all the others that have been tried.
Winston Churchill

Democracy means simply the bludgeoning of the people by the people for the people.
Oscar Wilde

Democracy is when the indigent, and not the men of property, are the rulers.
Aristotle

6

POPULAR SOVEREIGNTY

Popular Sovereignty is both a philosophy and a system of government. Many types of governments, including our own Democracy or Republic, purport to be a system of Popular Sovereignty.

In Popular Sovereignty systems power rests with the people, not the rulers. This type of government is based on a *social contract:* we will let you rule us if you have our best interests at heart, give us freedom, and protect our property and us. If you do not, we will invoke the philosophy of "Don't Tread On Me". We will put you out of power, and put someone in to govern that will do those things.

The notion of Popular Sovereignty can be found in the works of John Locke, Thomas Hobbs, and others.

Democracies all claim to be based on Popular Sovereignty. Even Dictatorships that act with benevolence claim to be a type of Popular Sovereignty. If the King or Dictator is not acting in the peoples interests, out he or she goes, often by rather unfriendly means.

7

AUTHORITARIANISM

—⁕—

The term Authoritarianism means a government by the one or the few that govern with no accountability to the people they are governing. In some cases the leader may be a "Strongman" like Hitler, or Saddam Hussein. In other cases, the ruler may be royalty, other aristocracy, or a religious leader or leaders. Sometimes, the Authoritarian leader (or leaders) rule from behind the scenes, and there is a "puppet" that is portrayed as the ruler for the world's consumption.

Many nations that are Authoritarian, have gone to great lengths to appear Democratic. They hold elections (the results are never in doubt) and may even allow opposition groups or parties (that really have no chance of winning an "election", but best act and say that they do).

PART II

A SMALL CLUB OF RULERS

8

ONE -PARTY RULE

—ᨇ—

One-Party rule describes a system of government that allows only one party to exist or participate. In many cases, it may be possible for other parties to exist, but onerous rules are set up to make it virtually impossible for a competing party or parties to participate in government.

Examples of One-Party rule would be the old Soviet Union, and present day Cuba. In the old Soviet Union, the Communist party controlled the leader. In Cuba, the leader controls the party.

North Korea is also a current example of a country with One-Party rule. So little is known about the "Hermit Kingdom" that it is not really known if the party controls the leader, or the leader controls the party.

In the United States, at the State level, a state with a Governor of one party that has a legislature with a strong majority of his or her party is often referred to as a state with One-Party rule. This usage of the term is not accurate, in that the other party has a right to exist, and actually could, theoretically, win an election.

One-Party systems exist in countries where a single party is extremely dominant for a long period of time. A good example of this in recent times would be our neighbor to the south, Mexico, where one party was in control for seventy years.

9

FASCISM

Fascist!! That is a name you call someone when you are in an argument and you are really mad. Or, it is a name you call a politician when that politician is perceived as trampling over your rights. Fascism is a pejorative term because it has been historically associated with three very brutal people: The Spanish Dictator Generalissimo Francisco Franco, Italian Dictator Benito Mussolini (who coined the term Fascist), and a man that needs no introduction-Adolf Hitler.

No doubt the three named above were very evil people. It must be pointed out that Fascism, as a philosophy, though it no longer exists anywhere in the world, is not really what most people think it is. Most people believe the term to mean an oppressive form of government headed by a ruthless Dictator.
Given that this word is associated with the three nefarious people listed above, this is not surprising. Fascism is something different, however, when it plays out without the ruthless Dictator (which is not meant to mean that it could be a good thing).

Mussolini himself, the man that coined the term, said that
"Fascism should rightly be called corporatism, as it is a merger of corporate and government power."

Under a Fascist government people have no rights and are expected to serve the needs of the state in a corporate-like fashion. Fascist governments are very nationalistic, xenophobic, and militaristic.

Fascism exists nowhere in the world today.

10

TOTALITARIANISM

Totalitarianism is a term for a state that seeks to control everything: where you live, what media you have access to (if any), where you work, when-where-if you travel, what organizations you may belong to, and even what you think or say. Such an oppressive state existed in literature in the novel *1984,* and exists in the world today in North Korea.

A Totalitarian state seeks to limit its citizen's contact with the outside world in an effort to stay in power and lessen any chance of dissent. In today's world, it is increasingly difficult to be Totalitarian. As a result, Totalitarian states tend to become Authoritarian states.

11

NAZISM

—⚇—

Calling someone a Nazi is also a very strong insult, given that it is associated with Adolf Hitler, the leader of World War II Germany and its Nazi party. The term Nazi comes from the abbreviation of the group National Socialistic German Workers Party (*Nationalsozialistische Deutsche Abeiterpartel*) the party of Adolf Hitler.

Nazism is a variant of Totalitarianism and is very similar to Fascism. It has the added components of strong Nationalism, racial and ethnic prejudice, expansionism, and militarism.

Today, the term is often used to describe White Supremacists, people who have strong agreements with the Nazi beliefs of Adolf Hitler. (Sometimes this group and similar groups are referred to as Neo-Nazis.)

12

PATRIMONIALSIM

—⁓—

Patrimonialism refers to the type of government where the interests of the ruler, or ruling family or *cabal,* are not different from the interests of the state. The ruler, or ruling family, basically owns the state, or most of its resources. The rulers control all the resources of the state. Those that help run the government owe everything they have to the ruler, ruling family, or ruling families.

Such systems are extremely Autocratic and are far from Democratic, though rulers in these systems often go to great extremes to appear Democratic.

Patrimonial systems typically do not change. Change may not be good for the ruling family or the ruler. Especially change that may modernize the country or empower the people.

In a Patrimonial system, the ruler expands his power to the point that there is no difference between his interests and the interests of the state.

Patrimonialism should not be confused with Praetorianism, a system of government where the military is of the opinion that they can run the state better than any civilians, be they elected or non-elected civilians. Prominent Praetorianism states in current times would include Pakistan under Pervez Musharraf, and currently Egypt.

13

THEOCRACY

—⚬—

A Theocracy can be defined as follows:

A government ruled by or subject to religious authority.
A state so governed.

A Theocracy is rule by God or his earthly representative. God's laws (as written in the Koran, Bible, Torah, etc) rule the land and are often interpreted by the priestly class. Historical examples include ancient Israel (governed by Mosaic Law) and early Islam as ruled by the Prophet Muhammad. At one time, even the Pope was a political ruler. From the fifth to the fifteenth century, European Kings justified their rule by "Divine Right".

Present day Iran may be a modern example of a Theocratic type state.

Hillary Clinton made the following statement about Theocracy and Iran:

You feel sometimes when you hear analysts and knowledgeable people talking about Iran that they fear so much about the survival of the regime, because deep down it's not a legitimate regime, it doesn't represent the will of the people, it's kind of morphed into kind of a military theocracy.

Robert Reich says of Theocracy:

We do not want to live in a Theocracy. We should maintain that barrier and government has no business telling someone what they ought to believe or how they should conduct their private lives.

PART III

A LOT OF FOLKS IN CHARGE

14

ANARCHISM

Anarchism subscribes to Henry David Thoreau's belief "that government is best which governs not at all."

Anarchists tend to have an extreme philosophy, that no one has dominion over them. That it is not fair for them to have to obey traffic laws, or any laws, for that matter. The government has no authority, moral or otherwise, over them. They totally reject the social contract that people submit to authority if that authority provides order and looks after their interests.

Anarchy is more of a philosophy, a fringe one at that, than a system of government. In fact the ultimate wish of the extreme Anarchist is that there is no recognized authority at all.

Anarchist movements have existed in many countries over the years.

There are two interesting quotes about Anarchism:

If man asks for many laws it is only because he is sure that his neighbor needs them; privately he is an unphilosophical anarchist, and thinks laws in his own case superfluous.
-Will Durant

We started off trying to set up a small anarchist community, but people wouldn't obey the rules.
-Alan Bennett

15

REPRESENTATIONAL DEMOCRACY

—m—

Total Democracy is not practical or possible. Total Democracy would allow for all citizens to have a direct role in running a country. People would not have the time or inclination to do so, even in a small Democracy as in Iceland. Certainly, in a large Democracy such as the United States (or India with over a Billion people) a true and full Democracy is impossible.

Instead, we have Representational Democracy. We elect politicians to represent our needs, and make decisions for us. We hope they will take our best interests at heart.

A Representational Democracy is reliant upon Political Parties. These parties lay out a clear vision for their country to attract support from voters.

Many Representative Democracies have several major parties. The United States has only two major parties. In the United States, the two major parties have a vested interest in making it difficult for a "Third Party" to gain traction. Because of this, the major parties often do what they can to make it difficult for a Third Party to compete, and often will appropriate ideas from those Third Parties to lessen their attractiveness to the voters.

16

RULE BY THE MAJORITY
MAJORITARIANISM

—⁓—

Majoritarianism is a philosophy that suggests that a government ought to do what majorities of the people want it to do. There are some problems with this, however. What if majorities of people want significantly lower taxes, to not have a deficit, and want to greatly improve public schools, transportation, infrastructure, and increase public housing. You cannot do all of these things.

What if a vast majority of people want to take away right of an ethnic or religious minority?

The majority of people want free speech, but does that mean someone can go on television and say untrue things about someone, knowing they are untrue and ruin their reputation, or even put their safety at risk while knowingly telling lies about them?

Such are the difficulties of Majority rule.

It is important that the wishes of the majority are not only ethical, but legal and moral as well. Under Majoritarianism, it is important that the rights of minorities be respected and valued.

17

CONSERVATISM

—◠◠—

Conservatism is a political philosophy that values the past, especially what has worked in the past. People with a Conservative viewpoint are sometimes thought to be more backward looking than forward looking (at least by their critics).

Conservatives rely intellectually on what has worked in the past, and often are hesitant to attempt new approaches.

Conservatives exist in all countries, not just the United States.

Conservatives also, in many cases, tend to be nationalistic, believe in a strong defense, value self-reliance and personal responsibility, and stress the importance of virtues. Religion is often important to Conservatives as well.

Prominent Conservatives in the twentieth century included United States President Ronald Reagan, and British Prime Minister Margaret Thatcher.

18

LIBERALISM

Liberals also exist in all countries. Liberals feel that "we are all in this together". People with a Liberal philosophy believe that government should be very active in assuring equal opportunity, equal access, and equal rights for all. There is also a feeling that the government should actively protect the populace from everything from unsafe food to natural disasters. Government exists to protect and watch over us in a benign way.

The Liberal philosophy also values the importance of a "strong safety net" to help the disadvantaged.

One of the more prominent Liberals in American history was Franklin Roosevelt.

In the United States many Democrats view themselves as Liberals (and many Republicans self identify as Conservatives).

19

SOCIAL DEMOCRACY

—ᘉ—

A Social Democracy is a form of Democratic Representative Government where the state tends to be heavily involved in the economy. To a degree then, Social Democracy is a term used in both Economics and Political Science.

In a Social Democracy the government may own in whole or in part businesses in key industries such as communication, power, gas, airlines, mining, and the like. What industries the government does not own outright (for the benefit of the citizens) it may regulate very heavily to make sure consumers are safe, treated fairly, and are not take advantage of.

Social Democracies often provide an array of social services for the citizenry. As a result, taxes often tend to be high, but services are more plentiful than they are in other Democracies.

Critics of Social Democracies decry their "Nanny State" involvement in the affairs of the nations residents. Critics also suggest that state controlled businesses are usually not competitive, as they do not have to be as efficient as businesses in the private sector.

Margaret Thatcher of the United Kingdom was instrumental in changing Great Britain from a Social Democracy to a more "Free Market" Democracy. Her supporters credit her with making British industry more competitive. Her detractors suggest she abandoned the less fortunate among us.

20

LIBERTARIANISM

—⁓—

Clint Eastwood once said (not to an empty chair) this about being a Libertarian:

"I mean, I've always been a libertarian. Leave everybody alone. Let everybody else do what they want. Just stay out of everybody else's hair".

It is relatively easy to sum up what a Libertarian believes: The less government the better.

Libertarians are most certainly not anarchists they want a government to keep order; they just want that government to be as small and as unobtrusive as possible. Government should exist only to protect people from someone harming them or their property, punishing those that do these things.

Libertarians view government regulation of almost anything as intrusive, as an affront to our liberties. We should be able to watch out for ourselves.

Like any other political philosophy, there are extremes. In other words, you can be a mild Libertarian, or a full-fledged hard core Libertarian. You might believe that you can drive as fast as you want on a highway, that any speed limit imposed by the police takes away from your individual liberty. On the extreme end, you may believe that there should be no public libraries, or public schools. The government should not require people to pay for these things through taxes. If you want the services they provide, obtain them on your own dime.

Prominent American Libertarians include Robert Ringer, as well as Ron and Rand Paul.

The writer PJ O'Rourke once said: "giving money and power to the government is like giving whiskey and keys to a teenage boy". Ronald Reagan famously said, "The twelve scariest words in the English language are 'I am from the government, and I am here to help you' ".

21

PROPORTIONAL REPRESENTATION

In the United States we are accustomed to single-member districts, winner-take-all elections. All of our lives we have lived within a system where we elect members of our legislative bodies one at a time in small districts, with the winner being the candidate with the most votes. This system seems so right to us that proportional representation (PR) elections may at first seem strange to us. Adding to the confusion is the fact that there are many different types of PR systems utilized around the world. In reality, the principles underlying proportional representation systems are very straightforward and all of the systems are quite easy to use.

PROPORTIONAL REPRESENTATION: THE BASICS:

The basic principles of proportional representation elections are that all voters deserve representation and that all political groups in a society deserve to be represented in our legislative bodies in proportion to their strength in the electorate. In other words, everyone should have the right to fair representation in government.

In order to achieve this fair representation, all PR systems have certain very basic characteristics—characteristics that are different from the system currently used in the United States. First, they all use multi-member districts. Instead of electing one person in each district, as we do here in the United States, several people are elected. These multi-member districts may be somewhat small, with only three or four members, or they may be bigger, with ten or more members.

A second characteristic of all PR systems is that they divide up the seats in these multi-member districts according to the proportion of votes received by the various parties or groups putting forth candidates. So, if the candidates of a party win 60% of the vote in a 10-member district, they receive six of the ten seats—or 60% of the seats. If another party wins 20% of the vote, they get two seats, and so forth.

That, in brief, is how proportional representation works. Though all PR systems have the same goals of ensuring that all voters receive at least some representation and that all groups are represented fairly, various systems do have different ways of meeting these goals. It is helpful to see how different versions of PR systems work in actual practice.

Types of PR Systems

Party List Voting

Party list voting systems are definitely the most common form of proportional representation in use today. More than 75% of the PR systems used worldwide are some version of party list voting. It is the system used in most Euro Zone Democracies and in many newly Democratic countries such as South Africa.

How It Works In Practice

Legislators are elected in large, multi-member districts. Each party puts up a "slate" or list of candidates equal to the number of seats in the district. Independent candidates (candidates not affiliated with a political party) may also run, and they are listed separately on the ballot as if they were their own party. On the actual ballot, voters indicate their preference for a particular party and the parties then receive seats in proportion to their share of the vote. So in a ten-member district, if the Democrats win 40% of the vote, they would win four of the ten seats. The four winning Democratic candidates would be chosen according to their position on the list.

There are two broad types of list systems: closed list and open list. In a closed list system–the original form of party list voting–the party fixes the order in which the candidates are listed and elected, and the voter simply casts a vote for the party as a whole. Winning candidates are selected in the exact order they appear on the original list.

Closed Party List Ballot

Most European democracies now use an open list form of party list voting. This approach allows the voters to express a preference for specific individual candidates, not just parties. It is designed to give voters some say over the order of the list and which candidates get elected. Voters are presented with unordered or random lists of candidates chosen in party primaries. Voters cannot vote for a party directly, but must cast a vote for an individual candidate. This vote counts for the specific candidate as well as for the party. So the order of the final list completely depends on the number of votes won by each candidate on the list. The most popular candidates rise to the top of the list and have a better chance of being elected. Highest and next highest number of individual votes, they would ascend to the top of the list and be elected. This example is similar to the system in use in Finland and widely considered to be the most open version of list voting.

Open Party List Ballot

There are many different formulas for accomplishing the actual allocation of seats to the parties. One of the simplest seat allocation formulas is the called the "largest remainder formula." In this approach, the first step is to calculate a quota, which is determined by taking the total number of valid votes in the district and dividing this by the number of seats. If 100,000 votes were cast and ten seats are to be filled. 100,000/10 = 10,000–which is the quota. The quota is then divided into the vote that each party receives and the party wins one seat for each whole number produced. So if a party received 38,000 votes, which is divided by 10,000 to produce three seats–with a remainder of 8,000. After this first allocation of seats is complete than the remainder numbers for the parties are compared and the parties with the largest remainders are allocated the remaining seats. In the end all the parties end up with the number of seats that as closely as possible approximates their percentage of the vote.

Largest Remainder Approach to Seat Allocation

Mixed-Member Proportional Voting

Mixed-member proportional representation goes by a variety of other names, including "the additional member system," "compensatory PR," the "two vote system," or" the German system." It is an attempt to combine a single-member district system with a proportional voting system. Half of the members of the legislature are elected in single-member district plurality contests. The other half are elected by a party list vote and added on to the district members so that each party has its appropriate share of seats in the legislature. Those that support this system claim that mixed-member proportional voting (MMP) is the best of both worlds: providing the geographical representation and close constituency ties of single-member plurality voting along with the fairness and diversity of representation that comes with PR voting.

This system was originally invented in West Germany right after the Second World War, though since then it has also been adopted in several other countries, such as Venezuela. It is still one of the least used PR systems, but in recent years it has begun to garner a great deal of advocacy. In fact, it is now one of the more attractive systems being considered by those involved in electoral design. It most certainly is gaining traction. In part this growing attention is a result of MMP's unique claim to be a "compromise" between the two main rival systems. Recently, New Zealand abandoned its traditional single-member plurality system for MMP. Hungary, Scotland and Wales have also adopted this approach.

How It Works.

People cast votes on a double ballot. First, on the left part of the ballot, they vote for a district representative. This part of the ballot is a single-member district plurality contest to see which person will represent the district in the legislature. The person with the most votes wins. Typically half of the seats in the legislature are filled in this way. So in a hypothetical 100-member state legislature, the winners of these district contests would occupy 50 of the seats.

On the right part of the ballot—the party list portion—voters indicate their choice among the parties, and the other half of the seats in the legislature are filled from regional lists of candidates chosen by these parties. The party lists are closed in the German version. These party list votes are counted on a national basis to determine the total portion of the 100-seat legislature that each party deserves. Candidates from each party's lists are then added to its district winners until that party achieves its appropriate share of seats. If say the Democrats won 40% of the party list votes in the 100-member state legislature, they would be entitled to a total of 40 of the 100 seats. Since they already elected 28 of their candidates in district elections, they would then add 12 more from their regional party lists to come up to their quota of 40 seats.

Allocation of Seats in MMP

In the German version two electoral thresholds are utilized, either of which a party must overcome to be allotted seats in the legislature. A party must either get 5% of the nationwide party list vote or win at least three district races in order for it to gain any seats in the legislature.

Single Transferable Vote Or Choice Voting

This system of proportional representation is known by several names. Political scientists call it "the single transferable vote." It is called the "Hare-Clark system" in Australia. In the United States, electoral reform activists have taken to calling it "choice voting." Currently this system is used to elect parliament in Ireland. In Australia it is used to elect the federal Senate, as well as the legislatures in several states there. It is also the PR system that was used in a number of cities in the United States during the twentieth century, including New York, Cincinnati, Cleveland, and Boulder. It continues to be used today in Cambridge, Massachusetts for elections to their city council and school board.

How It Works.

All candidates are listed in the same place on the ballot. Instead of voting for one person, voters rank each candidate in their order of choice. So if you like Jones best, you would mark the "1" after his name. If you liked Smith second best, you would mark "2" by his name, and so on. You can rank as few or as many as you want.

Choice Voting Ballot

As the name "single transferable vote" implies, this systems involves a process of transferring votes. To understand how the transfer process works, it may be best to start out with a simple analogy. Imagine a school where a class is trying to elect a committee. Any student who wishes to run stands at the front of the class and the other student's vote for their favorite candidates by standing beside them. Students standing almost alone next to their candidate will soon discover that this person has no chance of being elected and move to another candidate of their choice to help him or her get elected. Some of the students standing next to a very popular candidate may realize that this person has more than enough support to win, and decide to go stand next to another student that they would also like to see on the committee. In the end, after all of this shuffling around, most students would be standing next to candidates that will be elected, which is the ultimate point of this process.

In the single transferable vote, votes are transferred around just as the students moved from candidate to candidate in the analogy. For the sake of simplicity, assume that there is a three-seat district in which six people are running for office. The first step in the process is to establish the threshold: the minimum number of votes necessary to win a seat. The threshold usually consists of the total number of valid votes divided by one plus the number of seats to be filled, plus one vote. The formula looks like this: Threshold = (valid votes/1+seats) +1 vote. So in our three-seat districts with 10,000 voters, a candidate would need 10,000/1+3 (which is 2,500) plus one more vote, for 2,501.

Diagram of Ballot Transfer Process

The second step is to count all the number one choices to see if any candidates have reached the threshold of 2,501. Say the Democrat Quinn has 2,900 voters and he is declared elected. But Quinn actually has 399 more votes than he needs to win. These votes are considered wasted if they stay with Quinn, so they are transferred to the second choices on the ballot. (There are several ways to do this, but we needn't get into those details here.) In the second count, we see the effect of this transfer. The other Democratic candidate, Madigan, gets 300 of those second choice votes, and the independent candidate, Smith, gets the other 99. The vote totals are now recalculated to see if anyone is now over the threshold. No one is, so the next transfer takes place. The candidate with the least chance to win is eliminated and his or her votes are transferred to their second choices. This candidate is Sampson, the Republican, and 500 of his votes are transferred to the other Republican candidate, Dains; and the other 100 votes are given to Daniels. Again the votes are recounted to see if anyone has reached the threshold. Dains has reached it with 2,800 votes and so she is declared elected. Once again her excess votes are redistributed to their second choices–200 to Graybeal, and 99 to Daniels. But still no one has reached the threshold, so again the lowest candidate is eliminated and those votes transferred. That candidate is Campbell, the Democrat, and 100 of his votes go to Graybeal, and 600 go to Daniels. This puts Daniels, the independent candidate, over the threshold with 2,698 votes, and she is the last one elected.

Ballot Count and Transfer Process

This transfer process is a bit complicated, so why does it exist? The transfer process was invented primarily to reduce the problem of wasted votes–votes that are cast but do not actually elect anyone. Plurality-majority systems routinely waste large numbers of votes and this is why they are prone to such problems as party misrepresentation, and the underrepresentation of political minorities, racial minorities, and women. The transfer process in STV is designed to ensure that the fewest votes are wasted and that the maximum number of people gets to elect a representative to office. It acknowledges that there are two kinds of wasted votes: votes for candidates that stand little chance of winning, and votes in excess of what a winning candidate needs. Transferring these votes to their next ranked choice makes it more likely that they will actually contribute to the election of a candidate.

Simpler Than They Look

Again, to American eyes, these various PR systems often appear at first to be overly complicated and difficult to understand. And while the mechanics of seat allocation can sometimes be complicated, the actual voting process is not intimidating at all and can be easily utilized by the average citizen. Voters do not have to understand all the mathematics of these systems to use them effectively. To use an analogy: you don't have to understand how all the electronic components in your car radio work in order to use it to find the kind of music you like.

The party list system, the mixed-member system, and the choice vote have all been used for decades in other Western democracies. Voters in these countries have had no trouble using these systems, as indicated by the very high voters turnout rates that these PR countries enjoy. It is fair to assume that American voters would easily master the use of these systems as well.

In a smaller nutshell: in a system of Proportional Representation the political parties receive about the same percentage of seats in the legislative body as they earned votes in the election.

PART IV

DEMOCRACY UNPACKED

22

DEMOCRACY

A quote from someone that has been "in the arena" can often be informative:

The best argument against democracy is a five-minute conversation with the average voter.
-Winston Churchill

As I would not be a slave, so I would not be a master. This expresses my idea of democracy.
-Abraham Lincoln

It has been said that democracy is the worst form of government except all the others that have been tried.
-Winston Churchill

Democracy means simply the bludgeoning of the people by the people for the people.-
-Oscar Wilde

Democracy is when the indigent, and not the men of property, are the rulers.
Aristotle

The spirit of democracy is not a mechanical thing to be adjusted by abolition of forms. It requires change of heart.
-Mahatma Gandhi

The ignorance of one voter in a democracy impairs the security of all.
-John F. Kennedy

Legislative Power
A key component of a Democracy is Legislative Power. Legislative power usually refers to the government's ability to make law. Parliaments, Senates, and Congresses are often law making bodies. In all Democracies, the Executive Branch (President, Prime Minister, and their officers) often has limited authority to make rules as well.

John Saxe famously said "Laws, like sausages, cease to inspire respect in proportion as we know how they were made."

Executive Power
A President, Prime Minister, or other such head of state heads the Executive Branch in a Democracy. The Chief Executive of a country is charged with the duty of carrying out the laws, but he or she has many other powers as well. The Chief Executive enforces the laws set forth by the Legislative Branch, and the Courts. Further, he or she is bound to defend, obey and implement what is set forth in the nations constitution.

Often, the Chief Executive of a country is the major spokesperson and actor when it comes to foreign affairs, conducting war, and the like.

Judicial Power
The Judicial Branch of government in a functioning Democracy is independent of the other branches of government. Their independence is crucial to the rule of law. In a Democracy, theoretically, "no man is above the law."

The Judiciary is charged with the responsibility of determining who has broken the law, and what consequences will be applied for their illegal actions. In some cases a jury may be involved, in other cases, a judge alone may make these determinations.

Checks and Balances
Checks and balances require the three branches of government (the legislative, executive, and judicial) to share power. The idea being that no one branch will be dominant, and that each branch will be independent. In the United States, our experience with the English Monarchy inspired the writing of Checks and Balances into our Constitution.

Separation of Powers
Each component of a Democratic country, (Executive, Legislative, and Judicial) are separate and independent. Rivals in a sense. This is especially

important in America where many people believe that too much power in a single person or entity threatens liberty.

Parliamentary Democracy

The United Kingdom is a good example of a Parliamentary Democracy. In such a Democracy the voters elect members of the legislature who in turn decide on who the Prime Minister will be. Unlike in the United States, elections in a Parliamentary system do not happen at mandated regular intervals. Though there is a maximum amount of time an elected leader can serve without reelection, there is no minimum time. Early elections can be set if there is a loss of confidence in the government, (in a Parliamentary system, the opposition is able to express a loss of confidence in the government but putting forth a no confidence motion. If parliament votes in favor of this motion, the government must resign or hold elections within a prescribed period of time after the successful no confidence vote) or if the ruling government feels they have a chance to easily win an election and expand their maximum time to rule.

Federalism

In a Federal System, power is divided between the National Government and territorial sub-divisions such as States, Provinces, or Territories. In a Federal System, the National government holds most of the power, but a significant amount of power is assigned to the sub-units.

Federalist states are prevalent in large nations such as The United States, Canada, Australia, and India. They are also common in nations that have significant internal divisions (differences in language, customs, religion, or ethnicity).

Federalism got its start at the Constitutional Convention in America in 1787. At the time, the States had too much power (under The Articles of Confederation) and the country was not functioning smoothly. A compromise was made: the Federal Government would become stronger under the new Constitution, though the States would be delegated certain powers.

Unitary State
A Unitary State is a Democracy that allows for the Central Government to have all the power. The Central Government can, however, delegate some powers to local regional governments as it wishes. A Unitary State would be the opposite of a Federal System.

The majority of Democratic nations in the world are Unitary States. In this respect, the type of Democracy we have in the United States is in the minority.

PART IV

COMMUNISM: A DYING SYSTEM

23

COMMUNISM

—⁓—

Communism, as a political philosophy or economic system, is virtually extinct. It exists only in North Korea and Cuba at present, two very closed and poor societies. It is important to reiterate that the term Communism really denotes both an economic philosophy as well as a system of government.

All variations of the Communist philosophy derive from the works of Karl Marx, and hence can be referred to as Marxist. Marxism has some basic tenants:

1. Property is the states; it cannot belong to individuals.

2. There should be no distinctions between the classes.

3. A Communist state should ferment and support the overthrow of Capitalist systems abroad.

Though Communism ideally promised to remove class distinctions on the basis of economics, it replaced it with other more repressive distinctions. For example, active members of the Communist party had a favored status.

Communism purports to eliminate inequality, poverty, and oppression, but has had a very poor track record in these areas.

A common joke in the old Soviet Union, when it was a Communist state, was as follows: "We pretend to work, they pretend to pay us." This humorous statement gets at a basic truth: without incentives (private property, pay for productivity, etc) motivation is often missing, and people, and their society, will not prosper. Historically, when Communist countries have gone into an economic tailspin, they have allowed for private ownership or business to follow a more Capitalistic path in an effort to stimulate the economy.

Communist nations often have precious little individual freedoms.

Communism comes in various forms, for example, Maoism, Trotskyism, and Leninism. All variations adhere to the basic Marxist tenants described above.

There are two terms the reader must understand to understand Communism.

1. Bourgeoisie: These are the owners of the means of production. They exploit the Proletariat (to be described below), forcing this class to overthrow them and install a Communist government.

2. Proletariat: This is the working class. To survive, they must sell their labor to the Bourgeoisie. They are exploited by this upper class and will eventually revolt against them.

PART V

ECONOMIC SYSTEMS
AND POLITICAL SCIENCE

24

ECONOMICS

—⁓—

POLITICAL SCIENCE IN A NUTSHELL

Political Science and Economics are closely related fields of study. So much so that Political Science is a relatively new term for what used to be called Political Economy.

There are some basic terms one must understand to have a basic knowledge of the importance of Economics in the field of Political Science. These terms are: Socialism, Capitalism, Keynesianism, Globalization, Mercantilism, Objectivism, and Neoliberalism. Let us take a look at each of these Economic ideas, and focus on their importance to the study of Political Science.

Socialism
Socialism is an Economic approach that advocates for public control (or largely public control) of the economy. In a socialist economy, it is common for the state to control major industries in whole or in part.

Capitalism
Private parties actively exchange goods with as little interference from the government as possible. Capital refers to the savings people have. They use this capital to invest in their businesses, and to buy goods and services from others. Capital is necessary for Capitalism to prosper. Paradoxically, in a Capitalist system, everyone works very hard to relieve others of their capital.

Keynesianism
Keynesianism is named after the theories of Economist John Maynard Keynes (pronounced cane). This school of thought suggests that sometimes government has to be a major player in the economy. If the economy is stagnant, the government can improve things by deficit spending and purchasing goods and services, building bridges and roads, and the like. Such an approach is the exact opposite of a laissez-faire policy, which is a policy that advocates as little government involvement in the economy as possible.

Globalization
Nations are becoming more and more interconnected as time goes on. Nations economic policies must take this into account. In an advanced

nation, workers should concentrate on producing things that they can produce more efficiently, and import goods from other less developed countries where less complex work can be done more efficiently.

Mercantilism
Mercantilism is an economic policy that advocates putting ones own nation first in all situations. It is a form of Economic Nationalism. Mercantile nations have sought to export more than they import, thus increasing the national wealth. Domestic industries are aided by the state and encouraged to export to increase the nations wealth. Imported goods are regulated or taxed in an effort to support indigenous industry and to maintain a favorable trade balance.

Mercantilism is best represented by the relationship the American Colonies had to Great Britain, and India's early relationship with Britain. These territories existed to enrich the British nation. Britain had to maintain a strong navy to be a successful mercantile nation.

Objectivism
Objectivism requires the government to be very limited, and for people to have as much freedom as is possible. People must be allowed to act in their own self-interest. Objectivism is laissez-faire government in the extreme.

Neoliberalism
Neoliberalism advocates for extremely limited governmental involvement in the economy. The market will regulate itself, and do what is in the best interest of the country. People, acting in their own self-interest, will allow an economy to prosper. We must allow "the invisible hand of the marketplace" to reign supreme, free from any governmental manipulations.

PART VI

FOREGN AFFAIRS

25

REALISM

Realism, in Foreign Affairs, refers to a philosophy that suggests that power counts. Nations will act in their own self-interests and use power (military, economic, and the like) to obtain what they want. There is not an international body that can really hold a powerful nation in check, unless that nation wants to be held in check. In short, a realist believes that power rules.

International institutions can play a role, to be sure, but when it gets down to it, those with the power do what they want. They may dress it up a bit, disguise it, and claim they are doing the right thing, but they will still act as they please.

A Realist then, does not rely on international organizations to enforce international norms.

26

CONSTRUCTIVISM

—⧖—

Constructivism is a school of thought in Foreign Affairs that holds that the international order develops due to the social interaction of states that are acting and relating to their own perceptions of the world order, and their own self-interests.

Constructivism, along with Realism and Liberalism, are the major theories of Foreign Relations.

27

IMPERIALISM

—⁓—

Imperialism involves a strong country dominating a weaker country and exploiting the resources of that weaker country. Great Britain, for example, has had such a relationship with its Colonies, which eventually became an independent nation, the United States. The British also had such a relationship with India.

The idea behind Imperialism is this: the strong nation not only dominates the weaker nation, it enriches itself at the poorer or less powerful nations expense.

Imperialism often leads to Mercantilism, a term discussed earlier.

"Cultural Imperialism" is a term in use in modern times. This refers to a situation in which the culture of a powerful state is dominant over that of the weaker state.

28

NEOCONSERVATISM

—⚹—

Neo-conservatism is a relatively recent, and almost entirely American view of Foreign Affairs. Neoconservatives believe that there are good and bad (moral and immoral) states, The United States of America being one of the good ones. It is appropriate for that moral state to aggressively support the establishment of Democracy around the world, and to use it's power and hegemony (dominance) to compel other nations to adapt it's more ethical views.

Neoconservatives are often Nationalistic, and frequently believe in the importance of military power, and the right to project it.

29

NATIONALISM

—⁓—

Nationalism involves a very deep identification of a people based on religion, ethnicity, race, language, or cultural history. There is most certainly a sense of "us". Unfortunately, Nationalism often leads to a sense of "them" as well, and can stoke feelings that may lead to war.

In some nations, when things are not so good domestically, the government or other people of importance will encourage feelings of nationalism, or resentment towards other countries, to take the focus of the people away from domestic issues. For example, in China, when things are not going so well economically, the government will stoke Chinese Nationalistic emotions by rehashing old Japanese war crimes from the Second World War. When this is done, most Chinese people will focus their Nationalistic rage towards Japan, rather than focusing on their own poor economy, domestic political malfeasance, etc.

Nationalism may actually cross national boundaries in some cases. For example, ethnic Kurds (a stateless people) live in parts of Iraq, Iran, and Turkey and often have more of a sense of allegiance to being a Kurd than to being a citizen of Turkey, Iraq, or Iran.

30

ENVIRONMENTALISM

—w—

Environmentalism movements are very active in all parts of the world. In some nations, the "Green Parties", have significant representation in Parliaments. Environmental politics cross international borders. Greenpeace, an Environmental organization, boast members and supporters in many nations.

All Environmental parties have some basic things in common:

1. Reducing pollution of the air, water, and various ecosystems.

2. Preservation of wetlands, wild areas, watersheds, farmland, rain forests, fisheries, and other important natural features.

3. Environmental fairness, or justice. People that farm responsibly can compete selling their produce with those that do not. Polluters are punished. Industries that foul the environment are held accountable.

Environmentalism will become more and more relevant as the impact of climate change becomes more relevant to the day-to-day lives of people.

The United Kingdom, Australia, and New Zealand have Environmental political parties that have been around a long time.

In 1997 The Kyoto Protocol, signed by 187 countries, addresses emissions by nations that contribute to Greenhouse gases. The signatories promised significant reductions in these emissions. Sadly, the United States did not sign this accord.

Al Gore, former Vice president of the United States, has been a prominent voice on environmental issues.

BONUS SECTION THIRTY TERMS YOU SHOULD KNOW

1

HUMAN RIGHTS

—⟋⟍—

When the United Nations began in 1945, every member agreed to recognize an important part of the UN charter: "promoting and encouraging respect for Human Rights and for the fundamental freedoms for all without distinction as to race, sex, language, or religion".

Human Rights, historically, has been an important issue:

1690-John Locke's seminal work *Two Treatises of Government* was initially published.

1776-The Declaration of Independence (included within this book) was written.

1789-In France the *Rights of Man and of the Citizen* was developed by the French revolutionaries

1945- The United Nations Charter was signed by all member nations. Human Rights were an essential tenant of this charter.

1948- The *Universal Declaration of Human Rights* was developed. This document stated, "Recognition of the inherent dignity and of the el and inalienable rights of all members of the human family is the foundation of freedom, justice, and peace in the world".

Thomas Jefferson conducted the most eloquent discussion of Human Rights in 1776 in the American Declaration of Independence *"all men are created equal; that they are endowed by their Creator with certain unalienable rights; that among these are life, liberty, and the pursuit of happiness"*.

The increasing powers and influence of multi-national corporations may be the next playing field in the battle for Human Rights. These large corporations can have tremendous influence on a countries politicians and leaders, and in some cases, see Workers Rights as an obstacle to corporate profits.

2

JUSTICE

—m—

Justice, as an important political and philosophical concept has been discussed for thousands of years. In the year 375 BCE Plato discussed his
doctrine of Justice as harmony. Aristotle, in approximately 350 BCE
stated that Justice involved treating like cases alike. In the sixth Century
CE, Emperor Justinian described Justice as the constant and perpetual will
to render to others what is due them. In more recent history, John Rawls,
in 1971 theorized that Justice is fairness, and in 2009 Sen made a case for
Justice to be viewed through a pluralistic prism.

Justice is indeed a very abstract concept. We may not be able to agree on how
to define it, but we know it when we see it. We also are aware of its absence.

Perhaps the Indian Economist (and Nobel Prize Winner) Amartya Sen
described Justice best in his 2009 book *The Idea of Justice*. In this book
he put forth a parable. Three children were arguing over who should be
given ownership of a flute. One child says he is poor, and deserves the flute
because he has no other toys to enjoy. Another child says she should have
the flute because she is the only one that knows how to play it. A third
child says the flute should be his because it was he who made it. Each
child in this parable has a good claim to the flute. How this argument is
decided is determined by the needs of each child, concern about poverty,
and a concern for the arts. Not an easy, or clear-cut decision, to make here.

Sen made the following statement about Justice: "*We don't
Begin by asking what a perfectly just society would look like, but asking what remediable
injustices could be seen on the removal of which there would be a reasoned agreement*".

John Rawls, an American philosopher, suggest in his book *A Theory of
Justice (1971)* that a social Justice system must include impartiality, and
favoritism towards no specific group. It must also address when and how a
system of Justice should depart form these two requirements.

This much is sure about Justice: the concept of Justice may differ from culture to culture, and from era to era. It is a changing concept. It is difficult
to define in a universally agreed upon manner.

3

EQUALITY

Important dates in the discussion of equality are as follows:

1690- *Two Treaties of Government* was published by Locke.
1776-The Declaration of Independence was published in the United States. Inalienable Human Rights were discussed in this document.
1960-The *Constitution of Liberty* was published by Friedrich Hayek

Equality before God was accepted long before the concept of Equality before men. In many parts of the world today, Equality before men is a pipe dream. There are castes, ruling families, and religious leaders that rule. Equality among men is often not even conceptualized in these countries.

In the modern world, when we speak of Equality, we refer to Equality of opportunity. Certainly, there is not equality of position and wealth because people have different levels of talent. In modern societies, Equality generally refers to Equality of opportunity. Everyone should have the same chance to utilize his or her talents. Equality of results isn't guaranteed. People will achieve different results based on their talents and efforts.

4

REVOLUTION

—⁓—

Revolution is a powerful word, and threat. A brief history of some world changing Revolutions include:

1789-1799-The French Revolution, a Monarchy is overthrown.

1848-Karl Marx publishes *The Communist Manifesto*

1917-The Russian Revolution ends the reign of the Czars.

1989-Communism in the Soviet Union (and Eastern Europe) collapses.

Karl Marx described Revolution as "the forcible overthrow of all existing social conditions". This definition presupposes that there must be an existing system, or old order, to overthrow. A Revolution must lead to a transformation into something, a new order.

Abrose Bierce wrote the following in 1906: "Revolution: an abrupt change in the form of misgovernment…Revolutions are usually accompanied by a considerable effusion of blood, but are accounted worth it-this appraisement being made by the beneficiaries whose blood had not mischance to be shed".

In 1970 political theorist Hannah Arendt stated "The most radical Revolutionary will become a conservative on the day after the Revolution".

Even the Beatles wrote a song entitled Revolution:

You say you want a revolution
Well, you know
We all want to change the world
You tell me that it's evolution
Well, you know
We all want to change the world
But when you talk about destruction
Don't you know that you can count me out
Don't you know it's gonna be all right
All right, all right

You say you got a real solution
Well, you know
We'd all love to see the plan
You ask me for a contribution
Well, you know
We're doing what we can
But when you want money
For people with minds that hate
All I can tell is brother you have to wait
Don't you know it's gonna be all right
All right, all right
Ah

Ah, ah, ah, ah, ah...

You say you'll change the constitution
Well, you know
We all want to change your head
You tell me it's the institution
Well, you know
You better free you mind instead
But if you go carrying pictures of chairman Mao
You ain't going to make it with anyone anyhow
Don't you know it's gonna be all right
All right, all right
All right, all right, all right
All right, all right, all right

5

SOCIAL CONTRACT

People make an implicit Social Contract with their government: The government can make rules regulating our behavior, enforce those rules, make war on our behalf, tax us, and regulate our behavior in many ways, if they save us from the anarchy and chaos that the absence of governmental authority would bring.

For hundreds of years, governments have been considered legitimate on the basis of this Social Contract.

We can best understand the importance of the Social Contract if we engage in a thought experiment, and imagine a world without government.

6

TYRANNY

—⁓—

It is time to revisit Tyranny as a term used in Political Science, not as a form of government.

Tyranny and Tyrant are words that are often used as insults in the world of politics today. If the President is not doing something you want him to do, or if he is doing something you would rather he not, it is easy to call him a Tyrant. After all, we live in a Democracy, shouldn't he be doing what we want him to do?

Despotism and Dictatorship are words that have a very similar meaning to Tyranny. Though Tyranny is a word with a lot of negative baggage today, it has not always been that way. To the ancient Greeks it meant someone who illegally seized power within the government. It referred to how someone came to power, not how they ruled. A Tyrant then, in ancient times, was a Usurper. They may well have gone on to be a good and compassionate ruler. Today, the term is quite synonymous with Dictator.

In present times, the term Tyranny is used in a negative way quite frequently. If you are in the minority party, and the majority party passes laws without a single vote from the minority party, or without addressing the concerns of the minority party, the majority party is often described as "the Tyranny of the majority" by those that are in the minority party.

Today, Political Scientists tend to agree that a Tyranny describes those that grabbed power illegally and do not obey the laws. It is largely indistinguishable from a Dictatorship.

7

SECULARISM

—ᵐ—

Secularism came about as a necessity for survival in Europe. In the early eighteenth century, Europe went through many religious wars. It was this that led to the development of Secular states. Though Europe now has Secular government, paradoxically there are state churches in the United Kingdom and the Scandinavian countries. Minorities in these nations have a right to religious freedom, and are not oppressed.

The United States has long had a wall between religion and government, the so-called separation of church and state.

In 1992 Supreme Court Justice Henry Blackmun wrote the following opinion on a case before the court dealing with prayer in the public schools:

"The mixing of government and religion can be a threat to free government... When the government puts its imprimatur on a particular religion, it conveys a message of exclusion to all those that do not adhere to the favored beliefs. A government cannot be premised on the belief that all persons are created equal when it asserts that God prefers some... When the government arrogates itself a role in religious affairs, it abandons its obligation as a guarantor of democracy."

Though the separation of church and state is valued in America, President Bill Clinton famously addressed a slightly nuanced version of this important principle when he said:
"THE FACT THAT WE HAVE FREEDOM OF RLIGION DOESN'T MEAN WE NEED TO TRY TO HAVE FREEDOM FROM RELIGION."

8

REPUBLICANISM

—ᴡᴡ—

The second President of the United States perhaps described Republicanism better than anyone before or since:

"*The true and only true definition of a Republic is a government, in which all men, rich and poor, magistrates and subjects, officers and people, masters and servants, the first citizen and the last, are equally subject to the laws*".

What John Adams meant is that Republicanism means that no man is above the law. In Adams time in many nations, the King *was* law. Republicanism was a reaction to this.

Thomas Paine famously wrote in his Pamphlet *Common Sense:*

In America the law is king. For as in an absolute government the king is law, so in free countries the law ought to be king."

9

CONSERVATISM

"If it ain't broke, don't fix it". These seven words provide an overly simplified definition of Conservatism. Conservatism values the tried and true over the new, and potentially not as good.

Here is how Abraham Lincoln described Conservatism:
"Adherence to the old and tried against the new and untried".

Conservatives are often quite nostalgic. Past practices, values, and history are valued. The knowledge of a society acquired over time must be respected.

Liberals often view Conservatives as Luddites of sorts, and as people that fear change. Conservatives feel that they value and respect what came before them.

Conservatives are a bit critical of human nature, and tend to believe in laws that will keep peoples baser instincts in check. Liberals have a more optimistic view of human nature.

Edmund Burke, a Conservative thinker of the eighteenth century, made the following statement about Conservatism:

"There is something else than the mere alternative of absolute destruction or unreformed existence...a disposition to preserve and an ability to improve, taken together, would be my standard of a statesman".

Matthew Arnold, a Victorian era political theorist that might best be described as Liberal, critiqued the Conservative philosophy by stating:

"The principle of Conservatism destroys what it loves because it will not mend it".

In the twentieth century Conservatism was embodied in Reaganomics in the United States, and Thatcherism in the United Kingdom.

10

LIBERALISM

—⁓—

Conservatives often bandy about the term Liberal in the United States in a negative way. In Europe, the word tends to be a compliment and refers to someone that is socially progressive and is a staunch defender of civil liberties.

John F. Kennedy may have described Liberalism best when he said:

"When the Democrats opponents use the label 'liberal', they wish to suggest someone who is 'soft in his policies abroad, who is against local government, and who is unconcerned with the taxpayer dollar'. 'But, a liberal is someone who looks ahead and not behind, someone who welcomes new ideas without rigid reactions, someone who cares about the welfare of the people'.

Classical Liberalism can be defined in the following manner:

Defense of the liberty and liberties of the individual against abuses of power, premised on a view of individuals as rational, autonomous agents, each of equal value and hence worthy of equal consideration.

The above description of Liberalism can be traced back to the works of John Locke and Thomas Hobbes.

The quintessential American Liberal is Franklin Delano Roosevelt.

11

MULTICULTURALISM

—⁓—

The human race has always been mobile. Over the centuries people have moved as single families or whole populations. Often these movements were involuntary. They occurred because of war, slavery, natural disaster, or because of better opportunities elsewhere.

When people move they bring with them their language, culture, customs, and religious beliefs. These things are in their mind. Often, they bring few if any physical possessions.

People that migrate on their own volition, often interact a great deal with those in their new culture. If a people have relocated as slaves, this interaction with the host culture is limited.

When a group of people immigrate their adaption to the new culture can vary. Some immigrants quickly shed old customs and beliefs and quickly try to assimilate into the new culture. Other groups of immigrants are slow to assimilate, retain their old customs, and mostly live along side their hosts.

As a general rule, it is expected that an incoming group assimilate, or blend in with the host culture. In very modern times, cultural diversity is something that is celebrated, and an incoming people and the host culture cherish the culture of the newcomers. This is especially true in the Western world.

In the 1800's over thirty million Europeans came to North America. A huge influx of people from many different cultures. At first they came mostly from Ireland and Germany, then they came from many other European countries. By and large, these new Americans assimilated very quickly. It was expected. Their integration into American culture, in retrospect, went quite well.

The Great Seal of the United States holds the inscription *e pluribus unum* (out of many comes one). This is indeed what happened, many new arrivals came, and they all became 'Americanized.'

As Americans have begun to embrace multiculturalism, our melting pot has become more of a salad bowl.

12

LABOR AND THE LABOR MOVEMENT

Do you like the forty-hour workweek? Prohibition of child labor? Extra pay for overtime? Stringent work place safety requirements? Not being harassed on the job due to your gender, race, or ethnicity? If so, whether you belong to one or not, thank a labor union.

In the United States, labor unions often play an active role in politics, supporting candidates that are receptive to unions and workers. Frequently, unions support Democratic candidates. In America, Democrats are often viewed as pro-union and pro- labor, and Republicans tend to be viewed as pro-business (especially "Big Business).

In some European countries, there are political parties with the term labor in their name. These parties are extremely pro-labor.

In 1965, Dr. Martin Luther King spoke of the important contributions of the Labor Movement, and Labor Unions, in changing the lives of the working class for the better.

President Abraham Lincoln said:

"The strongest bond of human sympathy, outside of the family relation, should be one uniting all working people of all nations and tongues and kindred's."

Labor Unions as a force reached their zenith in the three decades following the Second World War. This was true internationally, and coincided with more "left-leaning governments" that were elected around the world. This prompted a high degree of cooperation between governments and labor unions, and the institution of many pro-labor laws in the industrialized world. During this era, wages and working conditions improved. It was indeed possible for a union worker to raise a family with economic security and a middle class lifestyle guaranteed.

In the later part of the twentieth century, the globalization of businesses, led to many jobs being lost to low wage developing countries that were not unionized. This seismic shift weakened Labor Unions in the developed world, they lost many members, and a great deal of their bargaining power.

Now in the twenty-first century, the influence of Unions seems to be waning. This is in no small part due to the continued globalization of labor, and the election of more Conservative, pro-business government officials that are passing laws that are not as Union friendly as in the past.

13

FEMINISM

Feminism, the belief that women should have economic, political, and social equality with men is a relatively recent phenomenon in the western world. It is only in the last century and a half that laws placing women as clearly second-class citizens have been changed.

Below is a timeline regarding equal rights for women that is instructive of improvements that have been made in that time span.

1848
The first women's rights convention was held in Seneca Falls, New York. This document summarizes grievances and sets the agenda for the coming women's rights movement. There is a set of 12 resolutions adopted calling for equal treatment of women and men under the law and voting rights for women.

1850
The first National Women's Rights Convention takes place in Worcester, Mass., National conventions are then held annually (except for 1857) through 1860.

1869
May
Susan B. Anthony and Elizabeth Cady Stanton start the National Woman Suffrage Association. The goal of this organization is to achieve voting rights for women by means of an amendment to the United States Constitution.

Nov.
Lucy Stone, Henry Blackwell, and several others form the American Woman Suffrage Association. This group promotes and seeks voting rights for women through amendments to individual state constitutions.

Dec. 10
Wyoming then a territory passes the first women's suffrage law. The next year, women begin serving on juries for the first time.

1890

The National Women Suffrage Association and the American Women Suffrage Association merge to form the National American Woman Suffrage Association (NAWSA). State campaigns for voting rights ensue across the country.

1893

Colorado is the first state to adopt an amendment granting women the right to vote. Utah and Idaho follow in 1896, Washington State in 1910, California in 1911, Oregon, Kansas, and Arizona in 1912, Alaska and Illinois in 1913, Montana and Nevada in 1914, New York in 1917; Michigan, South Dakota, and Oklahoma in 1918.

1896

The National Association of Colored Women is formed, bringing together more than 100 black women's organizations. Leaders in this black women's movement include Josephine St. Pierre Ruffin and Anna Julia Cooper.

1903

The National Women's Trade Union League (WTUL) is started to advocate for improved wages and working conditions for women.

1913

Alice Paul forms the Congressional Union to work toward the passage of a federal amendment to give women the vote. The group is later renamed the National Women's Party. Its Membership pickets the White House and practices other forms of peaceful civil disobedience.

1916

Margaret Sanger opens the first U.S. birth-control clinic in Brooklyn,

1919

The federal woman suffrage amendment, originally written by Susan B. Anthony and introduced in Congress in 1878, is passed by the House of Representatives and the Senate. It is then sent to the states for ratification.

1920
The Women's Bureau of the Department of Labor is formed to collect information about women in the workforce and to promote good working conditions for women.

Aug. 26
The 19th Amendment to the Constitution, granting women the right to vote, is signed into law by Secretary of State Bainbridge Colby.

1921
Margaret Sanger founds the American Birth Control League, which eventually becomes the Planned Parenthood Federation of America in 1942.

1935
Mary McLeod Bethune organizes the National Council of Negro Women, a coalition of black women's groups that lobbies against job discrimination, racism, and sexism.

1936
The federal law prohibiting the dissemination of contraceptive information through the mail is modified and birth control information is no longer codified as obscene.

1955
The Daughters of Bilitis (DOB), the first lesbian organization in the United States, is started. The DOB originated as a social group, but later developed into a political organization to win basic acceptance for lesbians in the United States.

1960
The FDA approves birth control pills.

1961
President John Kennedy establishes the President's Commission on the Status of Women and appoints former First Lady Eleanor Roosevelt as chairwoman. The report put forth by the Commission in 1963 highlights

significant discrimination against women in the workplace and makes specific recommendations for improvement, including fair hiring practices, paid maternity leave, and affordable child care.

1963

Betty Friedan publishes her highly influential book *The Feminine Mystique*, which describes the dissatisfaction felt by middle-class American housewives with the narrow role imposed on them by society. The book becomes a best seller and energizes the modern women's rights movement.

June 10

Congress passes the Equal Pay Act, making it illegal for employers to pay a woman less than what a man would receive for the same job.

1964

Title VII of the Civil Rights Act bars discrimination in employment on the basis of race and sex. At the same time it establishes the Equal Employment Opportunity Commission (EEOC) to investigate complaints and impose penalties.

1965

In *Griswold* v. *Connecticut*, the Supreme Court strikes down the one remaining state law prohibiting the use of contraceptives by married couples.

1966

The National Organization for Women (NOW) is founded by feminists including Betty Friedan. The largest women's rights group in the U.S., NOW seeks to end sexual discrimination, especially in the workplace, by means of lobbying, litigation, and public demonstrations.

1967

Executive Order 11375 expands President Lyndon Johnson's affirmative action policy of 1965 to cover discrimination based on gender. As a result, federal agencies and contractors must take active measures to ensure that women as well as minorities enjoy the same educational and employment opportunities as white males.

1968

The EEOC rules that sex-segregated help wanted ads in newspapers are illegal. The Supreme Court upholds this ruling in 1973. Women are now able to seek high paying formerly male only jobs.

California becomes the first state to adopt a "no fault" divorce law, which allows couples to divorce by mutual consent. By 1985 every state has adopted a similar law. Laws are also passed regarding the equal division of common property.

1970

In *Schultz* v. *Wheaton Glass Co.*, a U.S. Court of Appeals rules that jobs held by men and women need to be "substantially equal" but not "identical" to fall under the protection of the Equal Pay Act. An employer cannot, for example, change the job titles of women workers in order to pay them less than men.

1971

Ms. Magazine is first published as a sample insert in *New York* magazine. The first regular issue is published in July 1972. The magazine becomes the major forum for feminist voices. Gloria Steinem becomes a major figure of the modern feminist movement.

1972

Mar. 22

The Equal Rights Amendment (ERA) is passed by Congress and sent to the states for ratification. Originally drafted by Alice Paul in 1923, the amendment reads: "Equality of rights under the law shall not be denied or abridged by the United States or by any State on account of sex." The amendment died in 1982 when it failed to achieve ratification by a minimum of 38 states.

Also on Mar. 22

In *Eisenstadt* v. *Baird* the Supreme Court rules that the right to privacy includes an unmarried person's right to use contraceptives.

June 23

Title IX of the Education Amendments bans sex discrimination in schools. It states: "No person in the United States shall, on the basis of sex, be excluded from participation in, be denied the benefits of, or be subjected to discrimination under any educational program or activity receiving federal financial assistance." As a result of Title IX, the enrollment of women in athletics programs and professional schools increases dramatically. Title IX involves much more than athletic participation.

1973

As a result of *Roe* v. *Wade*, the Supreme Court establishes a woman's right to safe and legal abortion.

1974

The Equal Credit Opportunity Act prohibits discrimination in consumer credit practices on the basis of sex, race, marital status, religion, national origin, age, or receipt of public assistance.

In *Corning Glass Works* v. *Brennan*, the U.S. Supreme Court rules that employers cannot justify paying women lower wages because that is what they traditionally received under the "going market rate." A wage differential occurring "simply because men would not work at the low rates paid women" is unacceptable.

1976

The first marital rape law is enacted in Nebraska making it illegal for a husband to rape his wife.

1978

The Pregnancy Discrimination Act bans employment discrimination against pregnant women. Under the Act, a woman cannot be fired or denied a job or a promotion because she is or may become pregnant, nor can she be forced to take a pregnancy leave if she is able to work.

1984

EMILY's List (Early Money Is Like Yeast) is established as a financial network for pro-choice Democratic women running for national political office. More women are elected to Congress as a result.

1986

Meritor Savings Bank v. Vinson, the Supreme Court finds that sexual harassment is a form of illegal job discrimination.

1992

In *Planned Parenthood v. Casey*, the Supreme Court reaffirms the validity of a woman's right to abortion under *Roe v. Wade*.

1994

The Violence Against Women Act tightens federal penalties for sex offenders, funds services for victims of rape and domestic violence, and provides for special training of police officers.

1996

In *United States v. Virginia*, the Supreme Court rules that the all-male Virginia Military School has to admit women in order to continue to receive public funding. It holds that creating a separate, all-female school is not sufficient.

1999

The Supreme Court rules in *Kolstad v. American Dental Association* that a woman can sue for punitive damages for sex discrimination if the anti-discrimination law was violated with malice or indifference to the law, even if that conduct was not severe.

2003

In *Nevada Department of Human Resources v. Hibbs*, the Supreme Court rules that states can be sued in federal court for violations of the Family Leave Medical Act.

2005

In *Jackson v. Birmingham Board of Education*, the Supreme Court rules that Title IX, which prohibits discrimination based on sex, also inherently prohibits disciplining someone for complaining about sex-based discrimination. It also holds that this is the case even when the person complaining is not among those being discriminated against.

2006

The Supreme Court upholds the ban on the "partial-birth" abortion procedure. The ruling, 5–4, which upholds the Partial-Birth Abortion Ban Act, a federal law passed in 2003, is the first to ban a specific type of abortion procedure. Writing in the majority opinion, Justice Anthony Kennedy said, "The act expresses respect for the dignity of human life." Justice Ruth Bader Ginsburg, who dissents, called the decision "alarming" and said it is "so at odds with our jurisprudence" that it "should not have staying power."

2009

President Obama signed the Lily Ledbetter Fair Pay Restoration Act, which allows victims of pay discrimination to file a complaint with the government against their employer within 180 days of their last paycheck. Prior to this law, victims (most often women) were only allowed 180 days from the date of the first unfair paycheck. This Act is named after a former employee of Goodyear who alleged that she was paid 15–40% less than her male counterparts, which was later found to be accurate.

14

ISLAMISM

Islamism is very important to understand in our current times.

Al-Qaeda, in 2008, indicated that the goal of radical Islam is:
"To establish the Shari' a Islamic State that will unite the Muslims of the earth in truth and justice."

Islamists then want to have laws and customs as close to the teachings of the Qur'an as possible. They want to reinstitute Shari' a (Islamic Law).

Islamists view the Western world as an impediment to this goal. They resent Western involvement in the Middle East, and Western support of Israel.

It is important to note that all Muslims are not radical Islamists.

15

FUNDAMENTALISM

—⟋⟍—

Fundamentalism, or Fundamentalist belief, can be found in any religion from any country. Fundamentalism exists when a group believes that they alone have the truth, others do not, and that it is their responsibility to impose their beliefs on others because that is the right thing to do.

Fundamentalism can exist in Judaism, Christianity, Islam, or in any other religion. Fundamentalists often believe that Secular society wants to end or limit religion.

16

GREEN MOVEMENT

The current issue of climate change is a good example of an area of concern for the Green Movement, and how the Green Movement intersects with politics.

Those in the various Green Movements believe that we only have one Earth, and that we had better take care of it or mankind will not have a future.

Climate change, sustainable resources, pollution, and the like are all Green issues. Many countries actually have Green (or Environmental) political parties.

Green Movements started, in earnest, in the 1960's. Their genesis was with groups of scientists, NGO's (Non-Governmental Organizations) and other environmentally conscious groups. Originally, they focused on limited issues, and now focus on many environmental issues.

The Green Movement now advocates for "Responsible Stewardship" of the earth and its resources.

In the 1960's scientists first began talking about human activity and its effect on global warming. In the early 1970's the term Green was first used in describing groups focused on protecting the environment. 1971 saw the beginnings of the Greenpeace organization. New Zealand spawned the first Green political party (Values Party) in 1972. In 1992 Sustainability was discussed at the United Nations.

Green Parties will become more and more important and influential as the environment degrades, and people suffer as a result. This suffering will involve deaths from air pollution caused by fossil fuel use, unsustainable fishing practices that will lead to scarce seafood, industrial damage to watersheds and farmland, and many other avoidable tragedies.

17

PROPOGANDA

Propaganda is persuasion. It is an effort to change or reinforce the attitudes and behavior of a target group. Politicians try to persuade you, candidates hire people to manage news and to put a favorable appearance on their candidate's actions. The military tries to intimidate the enemy. During times of conflict, governments attempt to promote patriotism. All of these things are Propaganda.

Since World War II, and the proliferation of mass media, Propaganda has become more important and more utilized by governments. Nations attempt to promote their causes by demonizing the enemy. Propaganda is practiced by all sides in a confrontation and often involves exaggerations, half-truths, inflammatory rhetoric, and even xenophobia. The United States, as all nations do, uses Propaganda to influence not only its people, but also the people of other nations. Prior to the entry of the United States into World War II, the US government often reported terrible atrocities by the nations that were soon to become enemies of the United States.

The word Propaganda is thought to have originated from the term *Congregatio de Propaganda Fide* (Congregation for Propaganda of the Faith) a missionary group set up by Pope Gregory XV in 1622 to expand the Roman Catholic faith. Prior to the twentieth century the term Propaganda usually referred to religious messages and attempts of persuasion. In more modern times, it generally refers to government's attempts to persuade people to take a certain point of view.

During the First World War, many nations started "Information Ministries". In the 1930's, many people in the Soviet Union were "erased" from the history books, and became "unpersons". During World War II Goebbels's Propaganda department controlled all aspects of German cultures. The United States in the Vietnam War and in the Iraq war initiated a campaign to "win the hearts and minds" of the Vietnamese and Iraqi public respectively.

18

THE MEDIA

The extent to which the Media (electronic and print) can influence elections has been hotly debated for years. Most would agree that the Media has some impact on elections. The Media, then, is a powerful (and necessary) force in a Democracy.

The Media also serves the function of keeping government honest. When government is not truthful with the populace, investigative reporters often bring this to light. Without the Media, Richard Nixon would have served two full terms as President.

The Media is so important to a Democracy that it is protected in the First Amendment:

Congress shall make no law respecting an establishment of religion, or prohibiting the free exercise thereof; or abridging the freedom of speech, *or of the press*; or the right of the people peaceably to assemble, and to petition the Government for a redress of grievances.

The Media can, in effect, set the agenda for public interest. What the Media chooses to cover, and how it covers it, can be a powerful determining factor in what the politicians attend to, and what the people demand of their government.

An historical timeline of Media is interesting to view:

1605-The first weekly newspaper begins in Antwerp.

1650-Leipzig boasts its first daily newspaper.

1920- A Detroit radio station hosts the first radio newscast.

1928-The first television news program is aired in New York.

1990's- Newspapers begin publishing online news.

19

POLITICAL PARTIES

—⁂—

In the Federalist Papers, James Madison suggested that there are many causes-religion, the charisma of a leader, politics, economics, that lead to people forming parties so that they can achieve goals that they could not otherwise achieve on their own. Madison saw one of the prime functions of government as being a regulator of and reconciler of the "various and interfering interests" of parties that form to seek their own interests at the expense of others.

In modern times, the party system provides the structural framework within which politicians work to realize the values and promote the interests of the people that elected them.

In a one-party system the party is the apparatus of government. In a multiple-party system, competing parties vie for votes to earn the right to govern and to set the societies agenda.

Multi-party systems do allow for minorities to have some representation, a voice in government.

H.L. Mencken famously said:

"Under Democracy one party always devotes its chief energies to trying to prove that the other party is unfit to rule-and both commonly succeed, and are right."

In modern times the Internet has allowed for new channels for political expression. This was once a monopoly for the political parties. Will this lead to a decreasing importance of the political parties?

20

CIVIL SERVICE

—⁓—

Civil Service simply put is the state's bureaucracy. From the local animal control officer, to the worker at the Department of Motor Vehicles, to the person that makes sure the meat you eat is safe, these are the people that are necessary for a modern complex state to function.

Civil Servants are the non-military employees of the government that administer the affairs of the state. The military, armed forces, police and judiciary are in a class of their own and are often not considered to be Civil Servants.

Civil servants can be employed by cities, counties, states, or even by the Federal government.

Though the Civil Service is often criticized, it is essential, and necessary. Other means of providing the services have frequently proven to be unsuccessful.

Politicians and citizens are often quite critical of the Civil Service, but certainly want all of the services that the Civil Service provides.

In the early part of the twentieth century, Civil Services expanded to meet the demands of their societies. In the later part of the twentieth century, in Thatcher's United Kingdom and Reagan's America, big government, the Civil Service, was reviled and cut. This trend appears to have continued in the first decade of the twenty-first century.

21

CONSTITUTION

—⁓—

"We the people of the United States, in order to form a more perfect union, establish justice, insure domestic tranquility, provide for the common defense, promote the general welfare, and secure the blessings of liberty to ourselves and our posterity, do ordain and establish this Constitution for the United States of America." -This is how one of the most important documents in history began, the world's oldest and most durable Constitution.

This document went into effect on June 21, 1788 after the ninth state ratified it. It has been in effect, though it has seen some changes, ever since. The United States is not the only nation with a Constitution. Many have followed suit. Here is a timeline of Constitutional history worldwide:

1689-The Bill of Rights is created in England. It puts forth the principle of limited government.

1787-The United States Constitution is signed at the Constitutional Convention in Philadelphia.

1791-The French Revolution produces a Constitution and Constitutional Monarchy.

1958-The Constitution of the Fifth Republic in France is adapted.

A Constitution is the political essence of a nation broken down into rules and put on paper. Though the U.S. Constitution is the world's oldest, the idea and word predated the United States Constitution. What was unique about the American Constitution is that it's political philosophy and rules were distilled into a single document.

The U.S. Constitution is plain and straightforward. As in most of the World's Constitutions, this document explains how the political apparatus will be set up and function, what procedures are to be followed, how authority is distributed in government and how it is limited, and how leaders are chosen.

Constitutions are usually the result of Revolution or Reform.

Though Constitutions are usually very straight forward, they do tend to have "hidden meanings." These "hidden meanings" must be interpreted so they can be applied. In the United States, this interpreting is the work of the Supreme Court. All nations with a Constitution have a body charged with the responsibility of interpreting the document.

22

THE UNITED NATIONS

The United Nations is the World's largest international organization, and some might say it's most successful. Its headquarters is in New York City. Important issues have been addressed through the United Nations-health, agriculture, economic and social reform, human rights, peace keeping missions, and environmental protection to name a few. The most obvious indicator of its success may be that there has been no Third World War.

Even critics of the UN, and there are many, have to admire its vision.

The preamble of the UN charter reads as follows:

-The peoples of the United Nations declare their determination:

To save succeeding generations from the scourges of war.

-To reaffirm faith in fundamental Human Rights

-To establish conditions under which justice and respect for the obligations of treaties and other sources of international law can be maintained.

-To promote social progress and better standards of life in larger freedom.

There are currently 193 member nations. The UN charter was signed in San Francisco in 1945.

23

REALISM

---m---

Machiavelli is, perhaps, the best-known Realist. Machiavelli suggested that it is better to be feared than loved. Today, a nation or leader that subscribes to Realism believes in national security, acting in ones own self-interest, and in not trusting other nations to be ethical or moral. Might makes right.

Neorealism, a current school of thought, states that all nations simply act in their own best interests.

Realism may be, in many ways, different from Optimism.

24

WARFARE

The Prussian Military theorist Karl von Clausewitz famously stated:

"War is the continuation of politics by other means."

Most theorists believe War to be woven in to our species DNA. Some believe that a mankind without War is possible.

Many people, including religious leaders, are of the belief that there is such thing as a "just war."

Most of the World's nations have signed on to the Geneva Conventions, which spell out the rules of war.

Ben Franklin once stated:

"There never was a good war, or a bad peace."

Otto Von Bismarck famously said:

"Anyone who has ever looked into the eyes of a soldier dying on the battlefield will think hard before starting a war."

An historical timeline of thought about War is instructive:

4th Century BCE-Sun Tzu writes *The Art of War* the first book on military theory.
5th Century AD-St. Augustine writes of the Christian Theory of Just War.
13th Century AD-St. Thomas Aquinas continues an explanation for Just War.
1832 AD-Clausewitz writes *On War.*

In modern times most leaders believe that a country should view war as a last resort, and only embark towards an armed conflict, even a just one, if there is a reasonable chance of success. It is immoral to ask people to sacrifice in vain. Proportional response to an adversary must also be considered.

25

NATIONALISM

—ᴧᴧ—

"A country is not a mere territory; the particular territory is only its foundation. The country is the idea which rises upon that foundation; it is the sentiment of love, the sense of fellowship which binds together all the sons of that territory."-Giuseppe Mazzini, one of the Italian leaders that helped bring about Italian unification.

Poet Samuel Taylor Coleridge wrote:

"I, for one, do not call the sod under my feet my country. But language, religion, laws, government, blood, identity in these makes men of a country."

Nationalism is certainly a force of unity, but it is also a cause of warfare.

26

ISOLATIONISM

—⁂—

We have enough problems of our own; lets not get involved with anyone else's. This pretty much describes the philosophy of Isolationism.

Isolationism is a relatively new term, being used for the first time in the twentieth century. After involvement in World War I, the American public lost its appetite for being involved in international affairs or alliances. Between the two World Wars, Isolationist feelings were very strong in the United States. Then came Pearl Harbor, and this sentiment all but disappeared. The perils of the Cold War may have put last nails in the coffin of Isolationism. Isolationism may be making a comeback of sorts in public opinion in the United States after wars in Afghanistan and Iraq as evidenced by strong public opinion against American involvement against Syria in 2013.

Isolationism has been endorsed as far back as George Washington who said:

"Tis our true policy to steer clear of permanent alliances with my portion of the foreign world."

In 1793 Washington issued a Proclamation of Neutrality. In 1801, Thomas Jefferson warned against "entangling alliances." In 1920 the Senate of the United States voted against U.S. membership in the League of Nations. Isolationism then, has a long history in our country.

Some nations are Isolationist not so much to avoid entangling alliances, but to keep knowledge of the outside world from their citizenry. North Korea would be an example of this type of Isolationism.

27

WELFARE

Most economists agree that the world has enough resources for all people to lead a comfortable life, but that wealth is spread unevenly. Welfare is basically a transfer of payments to those that are in need to lessen their plight.

After World War II, much of Europe, led initially by the United Kingdom and Sweden, set up social welfare programs to provide "cradle to grave security" for people. During the Great Depression in the United States, FDR pushed the "New Deal" to provide some security for people and some redistribution of wealth.

Lyndon Baines Johnson promoted his "Great Society" program to help the less fortunate.

Social Security, Medicare, Medicaid, Food Stamps, and the like are all examples of Welfare delivery.

Critics of Welfare suggest that it makes people dependent and unproductive. Supporters suggest it gives folks who, through no fault of their own, need assistance from time to time, and that a compassionate society should provide help.

Ronald Regan (US) and Margaret Thatcher (UK) did a great deal to limit Social Welfare in their respective countries.

28

POLITICAL CORRUPTION

—ᵐᵐ—

Political Corruption exists in all nations, rich or poor, first

World or Third World. It may involve a local Mayor demanding a bribe from a company to be awarded a contract to rebuild a cities sewer, or a Head of State expecting his son to be hired by a company that will be hired to build a road in the capital city. It could take the form of a Police Chief not enforcing laws for some consideration from the lawbreakers.

The harm of Political Corruption locally, nationally, and internationally is significant. This harm is most felt in developing countries where safeguards against Corruption are not as strong. In less developed countries bribes, extortion, and fraud can add significant costs to projects in a nation that has precious few resources already. A nation may have little to spend on infrastructure improvement. When a great deal of money has to be spent on bribes to win contracts that is money that is wasted. A culture of crime develops, and people loose respect for the government and for authority. This culture of corruption weakens the society as a whole, and can discourage foreign investment if foreign companies must "pay off" government officials to do business.

When President Barack Obama visited Kenya, he made the following comment about the rampant Corruption in that nation:

"Corruption…erodes the state from the inside out, sickening the justice system until there is no justice to be found, poisoning the police forces until their presence becomes a source of insecurity rather than comfort."

The costs of Corruption have a long-term negative effect on a nation. Customary bribes may be viewed as a way of getting business done, and a way of bypassing bureaucratic red tape, but this ingrained Corruption can hurt economies efficiency in the long term. When regulations that are there to protect the populace can be by-passed by a bribe, dangerous roads and bridges that are not safe and overpriced will be built.

In 1777 Edmund Burke addressed Corruption by saying:

'Among a people generally Corrupt, liberty cannot long exist."

29

POLITICAL CORRECTNESS

—ᴍ—

Language matters. Language used can impact people's feelings of self-regard, their aspirations, and even their status in a society. Discrimination is real. Many people that are denied opportunities are denied, in part, due to the language and customs of a culture. Political Correctness has much of its roots in the Woman's movement. Qualified women were not given opportunities to advance, and language used was deemed to be part of the cause. Soon, the term "Chairman" became "Chairperson". Change began to happen, and society was all the better for it (and more productive and efficient too).

Anything can be taken to extremes, however. "History" is not a pejorative term, and should not be relabeled "Herstory." It is these excesses that cause some backlash to Political Correctness.

Carrying Political Correctness too far, may lead not only to a backlash against it, but also to a slowing of social progress. Polly Toynbee, a British journalist addressed this danger when she wrote:

"The phrase 'Political Correctness' was born as a coded cover for all who still want to say Paki, spastic or queer, all those who still want to pick on anyone not like them, playground bullies who never grew up"

30

POVERTY

—m—

The huge gap between the rich and the poor is morally indefensible. Current data tells us that over 80 percent of the world's population makes do on less than ten dollars a day. The most impoverished 40 percent of people worldwide earn only 5 percent of global income, whereas the wealthiest 20 percent account for 75 percent of all income. Two Billion children live in the developing world. One-fifth of them do not have access to safe water, one-seventh does not have access to adequate health care, and one-third does not have adequate shelter. Every year, over ten million children die from malnutrition or preventable diseases. This is simply not moral.

Poverty exists even in the most developed of nations. Regardless of ones politics on Poverty, the following question must be asked: How long can a society or government survive when there is such unequal distribution of resources?

THE CONSTITUTION OF THE UNITED STATES OF AMERICA

—ᴍ—

PREAMBLE

We the People of the United States, in Order to form a more perfect Union, establish Justice, insure domestic Tranquility, provide for the common defence, promote the general Welfare, and secure the Blessings of Liberty to ourselves and our Posterity, do ordain and establish this Constitution for the United States of America.

ARTICLE I

SECTION. 1. All legislative Powers herein granted shall be vested in a Congress of the United States, which shall consist of a Senate and House of Representatives.

SECTION. 2. The House of Representatives shall be composed of Members chosen every second Year by the People of the several States, and the Electors in each State shall have the Qualifications requisite for Electors of the most numerous Branch of the State Legislature.

No Person shall be a Representative who shall not have attained to the Age of twenty five Years, and been seven Years a Citizen of the United States, and who shall not, when elected, be an Inhabitant of that State in which he shall be chosen.

Representatives and direct Taxes shall be apportioned among the several States which may be included within this Union, according to their respective Numbers, which shall be determined by adding to the whole Number of free Persons, including those bound to Service for a Term of Years, and excluding Indians not taxed, three fifths of all other Persons. The actual Enumeration shall be made within three Years after the first Meeting of the Congress of the United States, and within every subsequent Term of ten Years, in such Manner as they shall by Law direct. The number of Representatives shall not exceed one for every thirty Thousand, but each State shall have at Least one Representative; and until such enumeration shall be made, the State of New Hampshire shall be entitled to chuse three, Massachusetts eight, Rhode-Island and Providence Plantations one, Connecticut five, New-York six, New Jersey four, Pennsylvania eight, Delaware one, Maryland six, Virginia ten, North Carolina five, South Carolina five, and Georgia three.

When vacancies happen in the Representation from any State, the Executive Authority thereof shall issue Writs of Election to fill such Vacancies.

The House of Representatives shall chuse their Speaker and other Officers;and shall have the sole Power of Impeachment.

SECTION. 3. The Senate of the United States shall be composed of two Senators from each State, chosen by the Legislature thereof, for six Years; and each Senator shall have one Vote.

Immediately after they shall be assembled in Consequence of the first Election, they shall be divided as equally as may be into three Classes. The Seats of the Senators of the first Class shall be vacated at the Expiration of the second Year, of the second Class at the Expiration of the fourth Year, and of the third Class at the Expiration of the sixth Year, so that one third may be chosen every second Year;and if Vacancies happen by Resignation, or otherwise, during the Recess of the Legislature of any State, the Executive thereof may make temporary Appointments until the next Meeting of the Legislature, which shall then fill such Vacancies.

No Person shall be a Senator who shall not have attained to the Age of thirty Years, and been nine Years a Citizen of the United States, and who shall not, when elected, be an Inhabitant of that State for which he shall be chosen.

The Vice President of the United States shall be President of the Senate, but shall have no Vote, unless they be equally divided.

The Senate shall chuse their other Officers, and also a President pro tempore, in the Absence of the Vice President, or when he shall exercise the Office of President of the United States.

The Senate shall have the sole Power to try all Impeachments. When sitting for that Purpose, they shall be on Oath or Affirmation. When the President of the United States is tried, the Chief Justice shall preside: And no Person shall be convicted without the Concurrence of two thirds of the Members present.

Judgment in Cases of Impeachment shall not extend further than to removal from Office, and disqualification to hold and enjoy any Office of honor, Trust or Profit under the United States: but the Party convicted shall nevertheless be liable and subject to Indictment, Trial, Judgment and Punishment, according to Law.

SECTION. 4. The Times, Places and Manner of holding Elections for Senators and Representatives, shall be prescribed in each State by the Legislature thereof; but the Congress may at any time by Law make or alter such Regulations, except as to the Places of chusing Senators.

The Congress shall assemble at least once in every Year, and such Meeting shall be on the first Monday in December, unless they shall by Law appoint a different Day.

SECTION. 5. Each House shall be the Judge of the Elections, Returns and Qualifications of its own Members,and a Majority of each shall constitute a Quorum to do Business; but a smaller Number may adjourn from day to day, and may be authorized to compel the Attendance of absent Members, in such Manner, and under such Penalties as each House may provide.

Each House may determine the Rules of its Proceedings, punish its Members for disorderly Behaviour, and, with the Concurrence of two thirds, expel a Member.

Each House shall keep a Journal of its Proceedings, and from time to time publish the same, excepting such Parts as may in their Judgment require Secrecy; and the Yeas and Nays of the Members of either House on any question shall, at the Desire of one fifth of those Present, be entered on the Journal.

Neither House, during the Session of Congress, shall, without the Consent of the other, adjourn for more than three days, nor to any other Place than that in which the two Houses shall be sitting.

SECTION. 6. The Senators and Representatives shall receive a Compensation for their Services, to be ascertained by Law, and paid out of the Treasury of the United States. They shall in all Cases, except Treason, Felony and Breach of the Peace, be privileged from Arrest during their Attendance at the Session of their respective Houses, and in going to and returning from the same; and for any Speech or Debate in either House, they shall not be questioned in any other Place.

No Senator or Representative shall, during the Time for which he was elected, be appointed to any civil Office under the Authority of the United States, which shall have been created, or the Emoluments whereof shall have been encreased during such time; and no Person holding any Office under the United States, shall be a Member of either House during his Continuance in Office.

SECTION. 7. All Bills for raising Revenue shall originate in the House of Representatives; but the Senate may propose or concur with Amendments as on other Bills.

Every Bill which shall have passed the House of Representatives and the Senate, shall, before it become a Law, be presented to the President of the

United States; If he approve he shall sign it, but if not he shall return it, with his Objections to that House in which it shall have originated, who shall enter the Objections at large on their Journal, and proceed to reconsider it. If after such Reconsideration two thirds of that House shall agree to pass the Bill, it shall be sent, together with the Objections, to the other House, by which it shall likewise be reconsidered, and if approved by two thirds of that House, it shall become a Law. But in all such Cases the Votes of both Houses shall be determined by Yeas and Nays, and the Names of the Persons voting for and against the Bill shall be entered on the Journal of each House respectively. If any Bill shall not be returned by the President within ten Days (Sundays excepted) after it shall have been presented to him, the Same shall be a Law, in like Manner as if he had signed it, unless the Congress by their Adjournment prevent its Return, in which Case it shall not be a Law.

Every Order, Resolution, or Vote to which the Concurrence of the Senate and House of Representatives may be necessary (except on a question of Adjournment) shall be presented to the President of the United States; and before the Same shall take Effect, shall be approved by him, or being disapproved by him, shall be repassed by two thirds of the Senate and House of Representatives, according to the Rules and Limitations prescribed in the Case of a Bill.

SECTION. 8. The Congress shall have Power To lay and collect Taxes, Duties, Imposts and Excises, to pay the Debts and provide for the common Defence and general Welfare of the United States; but all Duties, Imposts and Excises shall be uniform throughout the United States;

To borrow Money on the credit of the United States;

To regulate Commerce with foreign Nations, and among the several States, and with the Indian Tribes;

To establish an uniform Rule of Naturalization, and uniform Laws on the subject of Bankruptcies throughout the United States;

To coin Money, regulate the Value thereof, and of foreign Coin, and fix the Standard of Weights and Measures;

To provide for the Punishment of counterfeiting the Securities and current Coin of the United States;

To establish Post Offices and post Roads;

To promote the Progress of Science and useful Arts, by securing for limited Times to Authors and Inventors the exclusive Right to their respective Writings and Discoveries;

To constitute Tribunals inferior to the supreme Court;

To define and punish Piracies and Felonies committed on the high Seas, and Offenses against the Law of Nations;

To declare War, grant Letters of Marque and Reprisal, and make Rules concerning Captures on Land and Water;

To raise and support Armies, but no Appropriation of Money to that Use shall be for a longer Term than two Years;

To provide and maintain a Navy; To make Rules for the Government and Regulation of the land and naval Forces;

To provide for calling forth the Militia to execute the Laws of the Union, suppress Insurrections and repel Invasions;

To provide for organizing, arming, and disciplining, the Militia, and for governing such Part of them as may be employed in the Service of the United States, reserving to the States respectively, the Appointment of the Officers, and the Authority of training the Militia according to the discipline prescribed by Congress;

To exercise exclusive Legislation in all Cases whatsoever, over such District (not exceeding ten Miles square) as may, by Cession of particular States, and the Acceptance of Congress, become the Seat of the Government of the United States, and to exercise like Authority over all Places purchased by the Consent of the Legislature of the State in which the Same shall be, for the Erection of Forts, Magazines, Arsenals, dock-Yards and other needful Buildings;-And

To make all Laws which shall be necessary and proper for carrying into Execution the foregoing Powers, and all other Powers vested by this Constitution in the Government of the United States, or in any Department or Officer thereof.

SECTION. 9. The Migration or Importation of such Persons as any of the States now existing shall think proper to admit, shall not be prohibited by the Congress prior to the Year one thousand eight hundred and eight, but a Tax or duty may be imposed on such Importation, not exceeding ten dollars for each Person.

The Privilege of the Writ of Habeas Corpus shall not be suspended, unless when in Cases of Rebellion or Invasion the public Safety may require it.

No Bill of Attainder or ex post facto Law shall be passed.

No Capitation, or other direct, Tax shall be laid, unless in Proportion to the Census or Enumeration herein before directed to be taken.

No Tax or Duty shall be laid on Articles exported from any State.

No Preference shall be given by any Regulation of Commerce or Revenue to the Ports of one State over those of another: nor shall Vessels bound to, or from, one State, be obliged to enter, clear, or pay Duties in another.

No Money shall be drawn from the Treasury, but in Consequence of Appropriations made by Law; and a regular Statement and Account of the

Receipts and Expenditures of all public Money shall be published from time to time.

No Title of Nobility shall be granted by the United States: And no Person holding any Office of Profit or Trust under them, shall, without the Consent of the Congress, accept of any present, Emolument, Office, or Title, of any kind whatever, from any King, Prince, or foreign State.

SECTION. 10. No State shall enter into any Treaty, Alliance, or Confederation; grant Letters of Marque and Reprisal; coin Money; emit Bills of Credit; make any Thing but gold and silver Coin a Tender in Payment of Debts; pass any Bill of Attainder, ex post facto Law, or Law impairing the Obligation of Contracts, or grant any Title of Nobility.

No State shall, without the Consent of the Congress, lay any Imposts or Duties on Imports or Exports, except what may be absolutely necessary for executing it's inspection Laws: and the net Produce of all Duties and Imposts, laid by any State on Imports or Exports, shall be for the Use of the Treasury of the United States; and all such Laws shall be subject to the Revision and Controul of the Congress.

No State shall, without the Consent of Congress, lay any Duty of Tonnage, keep Troops, or Ships of War in time of Peace, enter into any Agreement or Compact with another State, or with a foreign Power, or engage in War, unless actually invaded, or in such imminent Danger as will not admit of delay.

ARTICLE II

SECTION. 1. The executive Power shall be vested in a President of the United States of America. He shall hold his Office during the Term of four Years, and, together with the Vice President, chosen for the same Term, be elected, as follows:

Each State shall appoint, in such Manner as the Legislature thereof may direct, a Number of Electors, equal to the whole Number of Senators and Representatives to which the State may be entitled in the Congress: but no

Senator or Representative, or Person holding an Office of Trust or Profit under the United States, shall be appointed an Elector.

The Electors shall meet in their respective States, and vote by Ballot for two Persons, of whom one at least shall not be an Inhabitant of the same State with themselves. And they shall make a List of all the Persons voted for, and of the Number of Votes for each; which List they shall sign and certify, and transmit sealed to the Seat of the Government of the United States, directed to the President of the Senate. The President of the Senate shall, in the Presence of the Senate and House of Representatives, open all the Certificates, and the Votes shall then be counted. The Person having the greatest Number of Votes shall be the President, if such Number be a Majority of the whole Number of Electors appointed; and if there be more than one who have such Majority, and have an equal Number of Votes, then the House of Representatives shall immediately chuse by Ballot one of them for President; and if no Person have a Majority, then from the five highest on the List the said House shall in like Manner chuse the President. But in chusing the President, the Votes shall be taken by States, the Representation from each State having one Vote; A quorum for this Purpose shall consist of a Member or Members from two thirds of the States, and a Majority of all the States shall be necessary to a Choice. In every Case, after the Choice of the President, the Person having the greatest Number of Votes of the Electors shall be the Vice President. But if there should remain two or more who have equal Votes, the Senate shall chuse from them by Ballot the Vice President.

The Congress may determine the Time of chusing the Electors, and the Day on which they shall give their Votes; which Day shall be the same throughout the United States.

No Person except a natural born Citizen, or a Citizen of the United States, at the time of the Adoption of this Constitution, shall be eligible to the Office of President; neither shall any person be eligible to that Office who shall not have attained to the Age of thirty five Years, and been fourteen Years a Resident within the United States.

In Case of the Removal of the President from Office, or of his Death, Resignation, or Inability to discharge the Powers and Duties of the said Office, the Same shall devolve on the Vice President, and the Congress may by Law provide for the Case of Removal, Death, Resignation or Inability, both of the President and Vice President, declaring what Officer shall then act as President, and such Officer shall act accordingly, until the Disability be removed, or a President shall be elected.

The President shall, at stated Times, receive for his Services, a Compensation, which shall neither be increased nor diminished during the Period for which he shall have been elected, and he shall not receive within that Period any other Emolument from the United States, or any of them.

Before he enter on the Execution of his Office, he shall take the following Oath or Affirmation:—"I do solemnly swear (or affirm) that I will faithfully execute the Office of President of the United States, and will to the best of my Ability, preserve, protect and defend the Constitution of the United States."

SECTION. 2. The President shall be Commander in Chief of the Army and Navy of the United States, and of the Militia of the several States, when called into the actual Service of the United States; he may require the Opinion, in writing, of the principal Officer in each of the executive Departments, upon any Subject relating to the Duties of their respective Offices, and he shall have Power to grant Reprieves and Pardons for Offenses against the United States, except in Cases of Impeachment.

He shall have Power, by and with the Advice and Consent of the Senate, to make Treaties, provided two thirds of the Senators present concur; and he shall nominate, and by and with the Advice and Consent of the Senate, shall appoint Ambassadors, other public Ministers and Consuls, Judges of the supreme Court, and all other Officers of the United States, whose Appointments are not herein otherwise provided for, and which shall be established by Law: but the Congress may by Law vest the Appointment of such inferior Officers, as they think proper, in the President alone, in the Courts of Law, or in the Heads of Departments.

The President shall have Power to fill up all Vacancies that may happen during the Recess of the Senate, by granting Commissions which shall expire at the End of their next Session.

SECTION. 3. He shall from time to time give to the Congress Information of the State of the Union, and recommend to their Consideration such Measures as he shall judge necessary and expedient; he may, on extraordinary Occasions, convene both Houses, or either of them, and in Case of Disagreement between them, with Respect to the Time of Adjournment, he may adjourn them to such Time as he shall think proper; he shall receive Ambassadors and other public Ministers; he shall take Care that the Laws be faithfully executed, and shall Commission all the Officers of the United States.

SECTION. 4. The President, Vice President and all civil Officers of the United States, shall be removed from Office on Impeachment for, and Conviction of, Treason, Bribery, or other high Crimes and Misdemeanors.

ARTICLE III

SECTION. 1. The judicial Power of the United States, shall be vested in one supreme Court, and in such inferior Courts as the Congress may from time to time ordain and establish. The Judges, both of the supreme and inferior Courts, shall hold their Offices during good Behaviour, and shall, at stated Times, receive for their Services, a Compensation, which shall not be diminished during their Continuance in Office.

SECTION. 2. The judicial Power shall extend to all Cases, in Law and Equity, arising under this Constitution, the Laws of the United States, and Treaties made, or which shall be made, under their Authority;–to all Cases affecting Ambassadors, other public Ministers and Consuls;–to all Cases of admiralty and maritime Jurisdiction;–to Controversies to which the United States shall be a Party;–to Controversies between two or more States;–between a State and Citizens of another State;–between Citizens of different States;–between Citizens of the same State claiming Lands under Grants of different States, and between a State, or the Citizens thereof, and foreign States, Citizens or Subjects.

In all Cases affecting Ambassadors, other public Ministers and Consuls, and those in which a State shall be Party, the supreme Court shall have original Jurisdiction. In all the other Cases before mentioned, the supreme Court shall have appellate Jurisdiction, both as to Law and Fact, with such Exceptions, and under such Regulations as the Congress shall make.

The Trial of all Crimes, except in Cases of Impeachment; shall be by Jury; and such Trial shall be held in the State where the said Crimes shall have been committed; but when not committed within any State, the Trial shall be at such Place or Places as the Congress may by Law have directed.

SECTION. 3. Treason against the United States, shall consist only in levying War against them, or in adhering to their Enemies, giving them Aid and Comfort. No Person shall be convicted of Treason unless on the Testimony of two Witnesses to the same overt Act, or on Confession in open Court.

The Congress shall have Power to declare the Punishment of Treason, but no Attainder of Treason shall work Corruption of Blood, or Forfeiture except during the Life of the Person attainted.

ARTICLE IV

SECTION. 1. Full Faith and Credit shall be given in each State to the public Acts, Records, and judicial Proceedings of every other State. And the Congress may by general Laws prescribe the Manner in which such Acts, Records and Proceedings shall be proved, and the Effect thereof.

SECTION. 2. The Citizens of each State shall be entitled to all Privileges and Immunities of Citizens in the several States.

A Person charged in any State with Treason, Felony, or other Crime, who shall flee from Justice, and be found in another State, shall on Demand of the executive Authority of the State from which he fled, be delivered up, to be removed to the State having Jurisdiction of the Crime.

No Person held to Service or Labour in one State, under the Laws thereof, escaping into another, shall, in Consequence of any Law or Regulation therein, be discharged from such Service or Labour, but shall be delivered up on Claim of the Party to whom such Service or Labour may be due.

SECTION. 3. New States may be admitted by the Congress into this Union; but no new State shall be formed or erected within the Jurisdiction of any other State; nor any State be formed by the Junction of two or more States, or Parts of States, without the Consent of the Legislatures of the States concerned as well as of the Congress.

The Congress shall have Power to dispose of and make all needful Rules and Regulations respecting the Territory or other Property belonging to the United States; and nothing in this Constitution shall be so construed as to Prejudice any Claims of the United States, or of any particular State.

SECTION. 4. The United States shall guarantee to every State in this Union a Republican Form of Government, and shall protect each of them against Invasion; and on Application of the Legislature, or of the Executive (when the Legislature cannot be convened) against domestic Violence.

ARTICLE V

The Congress, whenever two thirds of both Houses shall deem it necessary, shall propose Amendments to this Constitution, or, on the Application of the Legislatures of two thirds of the several States, shall call a Convention for proposing Amendments, which, in either Case, shall be valid to all Intents and Purposes, as Part of this Constitution, when ratified by the Legislatures of three fourths of the several States, or by Conventions in three fourths thereof, as the one or the other Mode of Ratification may be proposed by the Congress; Provided that no Amendment which may be made prior to the Year One thousand eight hundred and eight shall in any Manner affect the first and fourth Clauses in the Ninth Section of the first Article; and that no State, without its Consent, shall be deprived of its equal Suffrage in the Senate.

ARTICLE VI

All Debts contracted and Engagements entered into, before the Adoption of this Constitution, shall be as valid against the United States under this Constitution, as under the Confederation.

This Constitution, and the Laws of the United States which shall be made in Pursuance thereof; and all Treaties made, or which shall be made, under the Authority of the United States, shall be the supreme Law of the Land; and the Judges in every State shall be bound thereby, any Thing in the Constitution or Laws of any State to the Contrary notwithstanding.

The Senators and Representatives before mentioned, and the Members of the several State Legislatures, and all executive and judicial Officers, both of the United States and of the several States, shall be bound by Oath or Affirmation, to support this Constitution; but no religious Test shall ever be required as a Qualification to any Office or public Trust under the United States.

ARTICLE VII

The Ratification of the Conventions of nine States, shall be sufficient for the Establishment of this Constitution between the States so ratifying the Same.

AMENDMENT I

Congress shall make no law respecting an establishment of religion, or prohibiting the free exercise thereof; or abridging the freedom of speech, or of the press; or the right of the people peaceably to assemble, and to petition the Government for a redress of grievances.

AMENDMENT II

A well regulated Militia, being necessary to the security of a free State, the right of the people to keep and bear Arms, shall not be infringed.

AMENDMENT III

No Soldier shall, in time of peace be quartered in any house, without the consent of the Owner, nor in time of war, but in a manner to be prescribed by law.

AMENDMENT IV

The right of the people to be secure in their persons, houses, papers, and effects, against unreasonable searches and seizures, shall not be violated, and no Warrants shall issue, but upon probable cause, supported by Oath or affirmation, and particularly describing the place to be searched, and the persons or things to be seized.

AMENDMENT V

No person shall be held to answer for a capital, or otherwise infamous crime, unless on a presentment or indictment of a Grand Jury, except in cases arising in the land or naval forces, or in the Militia, when in actual service in time of War or public danger; nor shall any person be subject for the same offence to be twice put in jeopardy of life or limb; nor shall be compelled in any criminal case to be a witness against himself, nor be deprived of life, liberty, or property, without due process of law; nor shall private property be taken for public use, without just compensation.

AMENDMENT VI

In all criminal prosecutions, the accused shall enjoy the right to a speedy and public trial, by an impartial jury of the State and district wherein the crime shall have been committed, which district shall have been previously ascertained by law, and to be informed of the nature and cause of the accusation; to be confronted with the witnesses against him; to have compulsory process for obtaining witnesses in his favor, and to have the Assistance of Counsel for his defence.

AMENDMENT VII

In suits at common law, where the value in controversy shall exceed twenty dollars, the right of trial by jury shall be preserved, and no fact tried by a jury, shall be otherwise reexamined in any Court of the United States, than according to the rules of the common law.

AMENDMENT VIII

Excessive bail shall not be required, nor excessive fines imposed, nor cruel and unusual punishments inflicted.

AMENDMENT IX

The enumeration in the Constitution, of certain rights, shall not be construed to deny or disparage others retained by the people.

AMENDMENT X

The powers not delegated to the United States by the Constitution, nor prohibited by it to the States, are reserved to the States respectively, or to the people.

AMENDMENT XI

The Judicial power of the United States shall not be construed to extend to any suit in law or equity, commenced or prosecuted against one of the United States by Citizens of another State, or by Citizens or Subjects of any Foreign State.

AMENDMENT XII

The Electors shall meet in their respective states and vote by ballot for President and Vice-President, one of whom, at least, shall not be an inhabitant of the same state with themselves; they shall name in their ballots the person voted for as President, and in distinct ballots the person voted for as

Vice-President, and they shall make distinct lists of all persons voted for as President, and of all persons voted for as Vice-President, and of the number of votes for each, which lists they shall sign and certify, and transmit sealed to the seat of the government of the United States, directed to the President of the Senate;–The President of the Senate shall, in the presence of the Senate and House of Representatives, open all the certificates and the votes shall then be counted;–The person having the greatest number of votes for President, shall be the President, if such number be a majority of the whole number of Electors appointed; and if no person have such majority, then from the persons having the highest numbers not exceeding three on the list of those voted for as President, the House of Representatives shall choose immediately, by ballot, the President. But in choosing the President, the votes shall be taken by states, the representation from each state having one vote; a quorum for this purpose shall consist of a member or members from two-thirds of the states, and a majority of all the states shall be necessary to a choice. And if the House of Representatives shall not choose a President whenever the right of choice shall devolve upon them, before the fourth day of March next following, then the Vice-President shall act as President, as in case of the death or other constitutional dis-ability of the President.– The person having the greatest number of votes as Vice-President, shall be the Vice-President, if such number be a majority of the whole number of Electors appointed, and if no person have a majority, then from the two highest numbers on the list, the Senate shall choose the Vice-President; a quorum for the purpose shall consist of two-thirds of the whole number of Senators, and a majority of the whole number shall be necessary to a choice. But no person constitutionally ineligible to the office of President shall be eligible to that of Vice-President of the United States.

AMENDMENT XIII

SECTION. 1. Neither slavery nor involuntary servitude, except as a punishment for crime whereof the party shall have been duly convicted, shall exist within the United States, or any place subject to their jurisdiction.

SECTION. 2. Congress shall have power to enforce this article by appropriate legislation.

AMENDMENT XIV

SECTION. 1. All persons born or naturalized in the United States, and subject to the jurisdiction thereof, are citizens of the United States and of the State wherein they reside. No State shall make or enforce any law which shall abridge the privileges or immunities of citizens of the United States; nor shall any State deprive any person of life, liberty, or property, without due process of law; nor deny to any person within its jurisdiction the equal protection of the laws.

SECTION. 2. Representatives shall be apportioned among the several States according to their respective numbers, counting the whole number of persons in each State, excluding Indians not taxed. But when the right to vote at any election for the choice of electors for President and Vice-President of the United States, Representatives in Congress, the Executive and Judicial officers of a State, or the members of the Legislature thereof, is denied to any of the male inhabitants of such State, being twenty-one years of age, and citizens of the United States, or in any way abridged, except for participation in rebellion, or other crime, the basis of representation therein shall be reduced in the proportion which the number of such male citizens shall bear to the whole number of male citizens twenty-one years of age in such State.

SECTION. 3. No person shall be a Senator or Representative in Congress, or elector of President and Vice-President, or hold any office, civil or military, under the United States, or under any State, who, having previously taken an oath, as a member of Congress, or as an officer of the United States, or as a member of any State legislature, or as an executive or judicial officer of any State, to support the Constitution of the United States, shall have engaged in insurrection or rebellion against the same, or given aid or comfort to the enemies thereof. But Congress may by a vote of two-thirds of each House, remove such disability.

SECTION. 4. The validity of the public debt of the United States, authorized by law, including debts incurred for payment of pensions and bounties for services in suppressing insurrection or rebellion, shall not be questioned.

But neither the United States nor any State shall assume or pay any debt or obligation incurred in aid of insurrection or rebellion against the United States, or any claim for the loss or emancipation of any slave; but all such debts, obligations and claims shall be held illegal and void.

SECTION. 5. The Congress shall have the power to enforce, by appropriate legislation, the provisions of this article.

AMENDMENT XV

SECTION. 1. The right of citizens of the United States to vote shall not be denied or abridged by the United States or by any State on account of race, color, or previous condition of servitude.

SECTION. 2. The Congress shall have the power to enforce this article by appropriate legislation.

AMENDMENT XVI

The Congress shall have power to lay and collect taxes on incomes, from whatever source derived, without apportionment among the several States, and without regard to any census or enumeration.

AMENDMENT XVII

The Senate of the United States shall be composed of two Senators from each State, elected by the people thereof, for six years; and each Senator shall have one vote. The electors in each State shall have the qualifications requisite for electors of the most numerous branch of the State legislatures.

When vacancies happen in the representation of any State in the Senate, the executive authority of such State shall issue writs of election to fill such vacancies: Provided, That the legislature of any State may empower the executive thereof to make temporary appointments until the people fill the vacancies by election as the legislature may direct.

This amendment shall not be so construed as to affect the election or term of any Senator chosen before it becomes valid as part of the Constitution.

AMENDMENT XVIII

SECTION. 1. After one year from the ratification of this article the manufacture, sale, or transportation of intoxicating liquors within, the importation thereof into, or the exportation thereof from the United States and all territory subject to the jurisdiction thereof for beverage purposes is hereby prohibited.

SECTION. 2. The Congress and the several States shall have concurrent power to enforce this article by appropriate legislation.

SECTION. 3. This article shall be inoperative unless it shall have been ratified as an amendment to the Constitution by the legislatures of the several States, as provided in the Constitution, within seven years from the date of the submission hereof to the States by the Congress.

AMENDMENT XIX

The right of citizens of the United States to vote shall not be denied or abridged by the United States or by any State on account of sex. Congress shall have power to enforce this article by appropriate legislation.

AMENDMENT XX

SECTION. 1. The terms of the President and the Vice President shall end at noon on the 20th day of January, and the terms of Senators and Representatives at noon on the 3d day of January, of the years in which such terms would have ended if this article had not been ratified; and the terms of their successors shall then begin.

SECTION. 2. The Congress shall assemble at least once in every year, and such meeting shall begin at noon on the 3d day of January, unless they shall by law appoint a different day.

SECTION. 3. If, at the time fixed for the beginning of the term of the President, the President elect shall have died, the Vice President elect shall become President. If a President shall not have been chosen before the time fixed for the beginning of his term, or if the President elect shall have failed to qualify, then the Vice President elect shall act as President until a President shall have qualified; and the Congress may by law provide for the case wherein neither a President elect nor a Vice President shall have qualified, declaring who shall then act as President, or the manner in which one who is to act shall be selected, and such person shall act accordingly until a President or Vice President shall have qualified.

SECTION. 4. The Congress may by law provide for the case of the death of any of the persons from whom the House of Representatives may choose a President whenever the right of choice shall have devolved upon them, and for the case of the death of any of the persons from whom the Senate may choose a Vice President whenever the right of choice shall have devolved upon them.

SECTION. 5. Sections 1 and 2 shall take effect on the 15th day of October following the ratification of this article.

SECTION. 6. This article shall be inoperative unless it shall have been ratified as an amendment to the Constitution by the legislatures of three-fourths of the several States within seven years from the date of its submission.

AMENDMENT XXI

SECTION. 1. The eighteenth article of amendment to the Constitution of the United States is hereby repealed.

SECTION. 2. The transportation or importation into any State, Territory, or Possession of the United States for delivery or use therein of intoxicating liquors, in violation of the laws thereof, is hereby prohibited.

SECTION. 3. This article shall be inoperative unless it shall have been ratified as an amendment to the Constitution by conventions in the several

States, as provided in the Constitution, within seven years from the date of the submission hereof to the States by the Congress.

AMENDMENT XXII

SECTION. 1. No person shall be elected to the office of the President more than twice, and no person who has held the office of President, or acted as President, for more than two years of a term to which some other person was elected President shall be elected to the office of President more than once. But this Article shall not apply to any person holding the office of President when this Article was proposed by Congress, and shall not prevent any person who may be holding the office of President, or acting as President, during the term within which this Article becomes operative from holding the office of President or acting as President during the remainder of such term.

SECTION. 2. This article shall be inoperative unless it shall have been ratified as an amendment to the Constitution by the legislatures of three-fourths of the several States within seven years from the date of its submission to the States by the Congress.

AMENDMENT XXIII

SECTION. 1. The District constituting the seat of Government of the United States shall appoint in such manner as Congress may direct: A number of electors of President and Vice President equal to the whole number of Senators and Representatives in Congress to which the District would be entitled if it were a State, but in no event more than the least populous State; they shall be in addition to those appointed by the States, but they shall be considered, for the purposes of the election of President and Vice President, to be electors appointed by a State; and they shall meet in the District and perform such duties as provided by the twelfth article of amendment.

SECTION. 2. The Congress shall have power to enforce this article by appropriate legislation.

AMENDMENT XXIV

SECTION. 1. The right of citizens of the United States to vote in any primary or other election for President or Vice President, for electors for President or Vice President, or for Senator or Representative in Congress, shall not be denied or abridged by the United States or any State by reason of failure to pay poll tax or other tax.

SECTION. 2. The Congress shall have power to enforce this article by appropriate legislation.

AMENDMENT XXV

SECTION. 1. In case of the removal of the President from office or of his death or resignation, the Vice President shall become President.

SECTION. 2. Whenever there is a vacancy in the office of the Vice President, the President shall nominate a Vice President who shall take office upon confirmation by a majority vote of both Houses of Congress.

SECTION. 3. Whenever the President transmits to the President pro tempore of the Senate and the Speaker of the House of Representatives his written declaration that he is unable to discharge the powers and duties of his office, and until he transmits to them a written declaration to the contrary, such powers and duties shall be discharged by the Vice President as Acting President.

SECTION. 4. Whenever the Vice President and a majority of either the principal officers of the executive departments or of such other body as Congress may by law provide, transmit to the President pro tempore of the Senate and the Speaker of the House of Representatives their written declaration that the President is unable to discharge the powers and duties of his office, the Vice President shall immediately assume the powers and duties of the office as Acting President.   Thereafter, when the President transmits to the President pro tempore of the Senate and the Speaker of the House of Representatives his written declaration that no inability exists, he shall resume the powers and duties of his office unless the Vice President and a majority of either the principal officers of the executive department or of such other body as Congress may by law provide, transmit within four days to the President pro tempore of the Senate and the Speaker of the House of Representatives their written declaration that the President is unable to discharge the powers and duties of his office. Thereupon Congress shall decide the issue, assembling within forty-eight hours for that purpose if not in session. If the Congress, within twenty-one days after receipt of the latter written declaration, or, if Congress is not in session, within twenty-one days after Congress is required to assemble, determines by two-thirds vote of both Houses that the President is unable to discharge the powers and duties of his office, the Vice President shall continue to discharge the same as Acting President; otherwise, the President shall resume the powers and duties of his office.

AMENDMENT XXVI

SECTION. 1. The right of citizens of the United States, who are eighteen years of age or older, to vote shall not be denied or abridged by the United States or by any State on account of age.

SECTION. 2. The Congress shall have power to enforce this article by appropriate legislation.

AMENDMENT XXVII

No law, varying the compensation for the services of the Senators and Representatives, shall take effect, until an election of representatives shall have intervened.

DECLARATION OF INDEPENDANCE

—⚬—

IN CONGRESS, July 4, 1776.

The unanimous Declaration of the thirteen united States of America,

When in the Course of human events, it becomes necessary for one people to dissolve the political bands which have connected them with another, and to assume among the powers of the earth, the separate and equal station to which the Laws of Nature and of Nature's God entitle them, a decent respect to the opinions of mankind requires that they should declare the causes which impel them to the separation.

We hold these truths to be self-evident, that all men are created equal, that they are endowed by their Creator with certain unalienable Rights, that among these are Life, Liberty and the pursuit of Happiness.–That to secure these rights, Governments are instituted among Men, deriving their just powers from the consent of the governed, –That whenever any Form of Government becomes destructive of these ends, it is the Right of the People to alter or to abolish it, and to institute new Government, laying its foundation on such principles and organizing its powers in such form, as to them shall seem most likely to effect their Safety and Happiness. Prudence, indeed, will dictate that Governments long established should not be changed for light and transient causes; and accordingly all experience hath shewn, that mankind are more disposed to suffer, while evils are sufferable, than to right themselves by abolishing the forms to which they are accustomed. But when a long train of abuses and usurpations, pursuing invariably the same Object evinces a design to reduce them under absolute

Despotism, it is their right, it is their duty, to throw off such Government, and to provide new Guards for their future security.–Such has been the patient sufferance of these Colonies; and such is now the necessity which constrains them to alter their former Systems of Government. The history of the present King of Great Britain is a history of repeated injuries and usurpations, all having in direct object the establishment of an absolute Tyranny over these States. To prove this, let Facts be submitted to a candid world.

He has refused his Assent to Laws, the most wholesome and necessary for the public good. He has forbidden his Governors to pass Laws of immediate and pressing importance, unless suspended in their operation till his Assent should be obtained; and when so suspended, he has utterly neglected to attend to them. He has refused to pass other Laws for the accommodation of large districts of people, unless those people would relinquish the right of Representation in the Legislature, a right inestimable to them and formidable to tyrants only. He has called together legislative bodies at places unusual, uncomfortable, and distant from the depository of their public Records, for the sole purpose of fatiguing them into compliance with his measures. He has dissolved Representative Houses repeatedly, for opposing with manly firmness his invasions on the rights of the people. He has refused for a long time, after such dissolutions, to cause others to be elected; whereby the Legislative powers, incapable of Annihilation, have returned to the People at large for their exercise; the State remaining in the mean time exposed to all the dangers of invasion from without, and convulsions within. He has endeavoured to prevent the population of these States; for that purpose obstructing the Laws for Naturalization of Foreigners; refusing to pass others to encourage their migrations hither, and raising the conditions of new Appropriations of Lands. He has obstructed the Administration of Justice, by refusing his Assent to Laws for establishing Judiciary powers. He has made Judges dependent on his Will alone, for the tenure of their offices, and the amount and payment of their salaries. He has erected a multitude of New Offices, and sent hither swarms of Officers to harrass our people, and eat out their substance. He has kept among us, in times of peace, Standing Armies without the Consent of our legislatures. He has affected to render the Military independent of and superior to the Civil power. He has combined with others to subject us to a jurisdiction foreign to our constitution, and unacknowledged by our laws; giving his Assent to their Acts of pretended Legislation: For Quartering large bodies of armed troops among us: For protecting them, by a mock Trial, from punishment for any Murders which they should commit on the Inhabitants of these States: For cutting off our Trade with all parts of the world: For imposing Taxes on us without our Consent: For depriving us in many cases, of the benefits of Trial by Jury: For transporting us beyond Seas to be tried for pretended offences For abolishing the free System of English Laws in a neighbouring Province, establishing therein an Arbitrary government, and enlarging its Boundaries so as to render it at once an example and fit instrument for introducing the same absolute rule into these Colonies: For taking away our Charters, abolishing our most valu-able Laws, and altering fundamentally the Forms of our Governments: For suspending our own Legislatures, and declaring themselves invested with power to legislate for us in all cases whatsoever. He has abdicated Government here, by declaring us out of his Protection and waging War against us. He has plundered our seas, ravaged our Coasts, burnt our towns, and destroyed the lives of our people. He is at this time transporting large Armies of foreign Mercenaries to compleat the works of death, desola-tion and tyranny, already begun with circumstances of Cruelty & perfidy scarcely paralleled in the most barbarous ages, and totally unworthy the Head of a civilized nation. He has constrained our fellow Citizens taken Captive on the high Seas to bear Arms against their Country, to become the executioners of their friends and Brethren, or to fall themselves by their Hands. He has excited domestic insurrections amongst us, and has endea-voured to bring on the inhabitants of our frontiers, the merciless Indian Savages, whose known rule of warfare, is an undistinguished destruction of all ages, sexes and conditions.

In every stage of these Oppressions We have Petitioned for Redress in the most humble terms: Our repeated Petitions have been answered only by repeated injury. A Prince whose character is thus marked by every act which may define a Tyrant, is unfit to be the ruler of a free people.

Nor have We been wanting in attentions to our Brittish brethren. We have warned them from time to time of attempts by their legislature to extend an unwarrantable jurisdiction over us. We have reminded them of the circumstances of our emigration and settlement here. We have appealed to their native justice and magnanimity, and we have conjured them by the ties of our common kindred to disavow these usurpations, which, would inevitably interrupt our connections and correspondence. They too have been deaf to the voice of justice and of consanguinity. We must, therefore, acquiesce in the necessity, which denounces our Separation, and hold them, as we hold the rest of mankind, Enemies in War, in Peace Friends.

We, therefore, the Representatives of the united States of America, in General Congress, Assembled, appealing to the Supreme Judge of the world for the rectitude of our intentions, do, in the Name, and by Authority of the good People of these Colonies, solemnly publish and declare, That these United Colonies are, and of Right ought to be Free and Independent States; that they are Absolved from all Allegiance to the British Crown, and that all political connection between them and the State of Great Britain, is and ought to be totally dissolved; and that as Free and Independent States, they have full Power to levy War, conclude Peace, contract Alliances, establish Commerce, and to do all other Acts and Things which Independent States may of right do. And for the support of this Declaration, with a firm reliance on the protection of divine Providence, we mutually pledge to each other our Lives, our Fortunes and our sacred Honor.

THIRTY QUESTIONS TO ASK

—⚏—

1. Is the United States a Constitutional Monarchy with the Justices of the Supreme Court acting as Monarchs?

2. Is it Democratic to have California represented by two Senators, and for Wyoming to also represented by two Senators?

3. In a Democracy, is it right that a President can be elected with fewer popular votes than his/her opponent?

4. Should the ERA have become a Constitutional Amendment?

5. Congress is so dependent on donations form PACS, Corporations, and other special interests for their reelection expenses. Is it no longer possible for them to represent their constituent's best interests?

6. What impact will the decline of Newspapers and Magazines have on our Democracy?

7. How important are the Sunday morning news shows to our Democracy?

8. Has our right to privacy been too eroded? Is this good or bad for our Democracy?

9. Are there some cultures in the world where Democracy is simply just not right? Are there some societies better suited to other forms of government that we may find distasteful?

10. Does our presidential primary system almost insure that more extreme candidates are selected as the party's nominee?

11. Does Iowa have an outsized influence on the selection of the presidential nominees? If so, should this be corrected?

12. Should corporations have the rights of people? What does this mean, and what are the implications of this philosophy?

13. Would government be more responsive if we had more than two major parties?

14. Has Gerrymandering become so efficient and effective that Democracy has suffered?

15. Has the time come where the Filibuster has outlived its usefulness?

16. Amendments have been repealed. Should there be some consideration to revising the Second Amendment? Repealing it?

17. Can laws, ethics, and moral consensus keep pace with technology? Is this a major legislative challenge of our time?

18. The Constitution has a sacred status in the American consciousness. Is it dangerous to hold a two hundred year old document so sacred to the point that it is considered treasonous by many to revisit it, revise it, or write a new one?

19. Is partisan cable television and talk radio contributing to the strength of our Democracy or weakening it?

20. What threat, if any, do large trans-national corporations pose to Democracy? To Human Rights?

21. Are "push-polls" enough of a threat to Democracy that some consideration should be given to legislating them out of existence? Would

such legislation itself go down the "slippery slope" of hurting the Democratic process?

22. Has the nature of the Social Contract that has legitimized government changed? If it has, how and why has it changed?

23. Would a new constitutional convention be too dangerous to undertake?

24. Should Gerrymandering be ended by legislation? Why, or why not?

25. In recent times, Labor Union membership has decreased. Is this good or bad for Democracy? For society?

26. Is a third party a possibility in the United States?

27. Will environmental concerns lead to a viable Green party in the United States?

28. Will the governmental shut down of 2013 lead to significant changes in government?

29. Have the 9—11 attacks permanently changed the policing powers of our government?

30. Has surveillance technology brought about a "1984" type state?

CPSIA information can be obtained at www.ICGtesting.com
Printed in the USA
LVOW12s1632290614

392206LV00021B/950/P